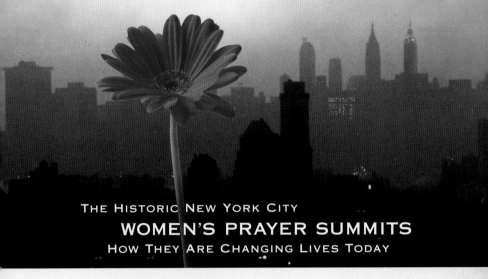

THE HISTORIC NEW YORK CITY
WOMEN'S PRAYER SUMMITS
HOW THEY ARE CHANGING LIVES TODAY

What Can One Woman DO?

Janet Broling

BRONZE BOW
PUBLISHING, INC.
Minneapolis, Minnesota

ISBN 1-932458-56-5

Published by Bronze Bow Publishing Inc.,
2600 E. 26th Street, Minneapolis, MN 55406

You can reach us on the Internet at www.bronzebowpublishing.com

Literary development and cover/interior design by
Koechel Peterson & Associates, Inc., Minneapolis, Minnesota.

Manufactured in Hong Kong

Contents

Acknowledgments

This book would never have been published without the prayer support, encouragement, and help from numerous people and groups—the list is almost too long to print. Ultimate thanks and appreciation go to my husband, Fred—to our children and their spouses, grandchildren, sister, brother, and niece. I am most fortunate to have special friends and I thank you—Dawn, Rob, Sallie, Gwen, and Jean, who have read and reread the book and helped with its writing and editing. Thanks to Kay who spurred me on and introduced me to the wonderful team at Koechel, Peterson & Associates, and their editor, Lance Wubbels. Their desires parallel mine—*to live to the praise of His Glory!*

Janet

Dedication

This book is dedicated in memory of my mother, the late Sally Thomas, and to all of you who co-labor with our Lord, as Mom did, through The Ministry of Prayer.

"Satan dreads nothing but prayer. The church that lost its Christ was full of good works. Activities are multiplied that meditation may be ousted, and organizations are increased that prayer may have no chance. Souls may be lost in good works, as surely as in evil ways. The one concern of the Devil is to keep the saints from praying. He fears nothing from prayerless studies, prayerless work, prayerless religion. He laughs at our toil, mocks at our wisdom, but trembles when we pray" (Samuel Chadwick, *E. M. Bounds on Prayer*, page 218).

Never stop praying. If God does not move you from the closet of secret prayer it is because of your inestimable value there. Through your prayers He will move others. Prayer works!

Janet

Introduction

October 4, 1997, New York City.

The Madison Square Garden rotating marquee on 7th Avenue stood still for one full hour with the flashing invitation:

JESUS BIDS US COME
to the Women's Prayer Summit

The flashing of the marquee was just a reflection of the vision that flashed through my mind as I knelt in prayer about 3:00 A.M. on Sunday morning, August 20, 1995. I saw a large assembly of believers, in a joyful, peace-filled atmosphere of indescribable glory. Now, after two years of countless miracles, here we were—in The Theater At Madison Square Garden—ready to hear from Him.

This venue has one of the most widely recognized names in the world. The walls of the arena have reverberated with the screams and cheers from the fans of boxing, basketball, famous celebrities, and politicians.

On this historic day, anticipation once again filled the venue. Today, however, the focus of the assembled was not famous men or women; the headliner was *Jesus*!

The message on the marquee was itself an answer to a dream. More than two years earlier, I had prayed that the secular marquees in New York City would display evidence of the strong faith in Jesus held by many people in this great city.

Unbelief almost kept that declaration off the marquee—I almost blew it! Four months earlier, when asked what message was to be placed on the rotating marquee, I hesitated. I wanted to put the words, *Jesus Bids Us Come*, but I feared rejection. I almost said something else, but the thought popped into my mind, *Give it a try*. I heard myself saying, "Please put *JESUS BIDS US COME,* followed by, *To The Women's Prayer Summit*, then the date and time." I nearly dropped the phone when I heard the reply, "Okay."

Every twenty minutes for four months, the marquee flashed the invitation, *JESUS BIDS US COME*, to the multitudes walking or driving by. Each time I saw the Name of Jesus and His call flashing upon the marquee, it filled me with gratitude to Christ for exchanging my apprehension with His boldness.

On this beautiful first Saturday in October 1997, women from numerous cultures, races, denominations, ages, and socioeconomic backgrounds responded to the invitation. They gathered together with one heart and one voice to help fulfill Jesus' garden prayer—the prayer He uttered in the Garden of Gethsemane—for complete unity in the Body of Christ:

> I AM NOT PRAYING FOR THE WORLD, BUT FOR THOSE YOU HAVE GIVEN ME, FOR THEY ARE YOURS. . . . MY PRAYER IS NOT THAT YOU TAKE THEM OUT OF THE WORLD BUT THAT YOU PROTECT THEM FROM THE EVIL ONE. . . . MY PRAYER IS NOT FOR THEM ALONE. I PRAY ALSO FOR THOSE WHO WILL BELIEVE IN ME THROUGH THEIR MESSAGE, THAT ALL OF THEM MAY BE ONE. FATHER, JUST AS YOU ARE IN ME AND I AM IN YOU.

—JOHN 17: 9, 15, 20–21

The women did not gather for a seminar, workshop, or performance. Instead, they came for a working meeting, to meet God Himself, to PRAY for His Spirit to prevail, and prevail He did!

In Dr. Robert Bakke's book *The Concert of Prayer*, he describes how one of America's greatest theologians, Jonathan Edwards, penned this dream in 1747: "If the union of praying Christians in 'different towns and cities' and in 'different countries' could be realized, 'who knows what it may come to at last?' Perhaps united prayers would even 'open the doors and windows of heaven that have so long been shut up, and been as brass over the heads of the inhabitants of the earth as to spiritual showers.' So taken was

Edwards with the vision of a unified Church literally covering the earth with harmonized praying, that he dedicated much of his energies throughout the last ten years of his life to promoting it."

What Can One Woman Do? tells the story of how God opened the doors and windows of heaven in New York City when His women heard and obeyed His plea to gather together in His Name and be as one. As you read of all the obstacles and improbabilities that God overcame to bring about this assembly, and of what He has brought about in the ten years following, my hope is that you will proclaim, "This transformation can happen in my family, in my church, in my city! These stories can be my stories! Lord, what do you want to do through me?"

CHAPTER ONE

The Garden Meeting

NO ELABORATE PROGRAM . . .

NO BIG NAME,

OTHER THAN JESUS.

ONLY THE PROMISE

OF HIS PRESENCE DREW THEM.

"Watch your language today, men!" boomed the union fore-man to all his employees in The Theater At Madison Square Garden.

This was the day's first proof of God's pleasure, and it came early in the morning of October 4, 1997. My heart pounded with excitement at the foreman's command. A year or so earlier, during a trip to the venue, language so vulgar that it turned my stomach had come from within an office. At that time, I asked, "Lord, do we have to put up with that?" No! We did not, and, we didn't even have to say anything—the Lord did it for us!

Two years of praying, fasting, planning, working hard, and watching as God opened hearts and doors had paved the way for this day. We could feel the electricity in the air! Each woman who had worked so hard and prayed so fervently for a manifestation of the Lord's glory was pulsing with anticipation of what was going to transpire. This day was her sacrifice of praise to her Lord.

Preparation for the sound equipment installation began at 8:00 A.M. and would not be ready for testing until 1:00 P.M. The program was scheduled to begin at 2:00 P.M! This required flexibility for all our musicians who needed to test the system in that hour, but it also worked to our advantage. The union allowed our choirs to practice right up until cur-tain time, which saved us considerable money. When the doors opened at 1:30 P.M. and the women came streaming in, they were welcomed with the beautiful live music coming from behind the huge closed curtain that separated the stage from the rest of the Theater.

The choir members were from all over the metropolitan New York City area—from different churches, denominations, and races. One would never have guessed that they had practiced together only a few times. A praise team of twelve women, equally diverse, provided additional harmony. The combination of the choir, praise team, piano, organ, and handbells seemed to resonate from the ceiling, walls, and floor of the Theater and sent chills down one's spine.

The women also walked into a well-oiled venue. Lydia and her prayer team began at 8:00 A.M. and walked aisle by aisle from the front of the Theater to the back. They stopped at each seat and prayed for every woman who would occupy it—that the Spirit of the Lord would touch her—that no one would slip through the cracks on this day.

LYDIA'S STORY

Lydia—a most extraordinary woman, a transformed woman of God—knew from firsthand experience the power of Jesus and the power of prayer.

She had lived the pain of heroin addiction and its ravages in her life at one time. She had been broken by her bondage. Driven by an insatiable need for the drug, she left her husband and family for the streets . . . and ended up in a psychiatric ward.

This was before Lydia met Jesus. While in treatment, she was introduced to her Redeemer, who changed her into a new woman. He freed her from the bondage and devastation of heroin and restored her family!

A spiritual mentor discovered that Lydia had never learned to read, so she tutored her. Lydia progressed rapidly and passed tests that gave her the equivalency of a high school education. She continued her education and for years worked for a major corporation in New York City. (At the time of this publication, retirement since 2002 has enabled her to travel to Africa, Europe, and cities in the United States to share her passion, teaching others of the transforming power of Christ through His Holy Spirit and prayer.) Lydia's unchanging passion led to the anointing of every seat and occupant with the symbolic oil of the Holy Spirit on this historic day.

Meanwhile, the Executive Committee, musicians, and all the other participants in the program were gathered backstage and prepared in prayer, waiting for the big velvet curtain to open.

No recognitions of titles or professional accomplishments of any of the participants would be announced (there could have been many). All had volunteered their time and gifts. This was an opportunity for Jesus' women to express their thanks, praise, and worship to Him through praying, singing, speaking, recording, translating, playing musical instruments, directing choirs or praise groups, composing songs and skits, praise dancing, acting, serving communion, and ushering.

At 2:00 P.M., a cross embedded in beautiful flowers on a floor-to-ceiling length banner emblazoned by the words, *Come to the Garden,* greeted the seated women as the curtain slowly opened. Pantomimes of Jesus and His disciples surrounded the banner and filled the stage. The worshiping disciples, some standing, some kneeling, were represented by members of the original fasting and prayer team. They had traveled from six states into the city to see and experience the realization of their prayers. Jesus was represented by one of our musicians.

The words of Christ's last prayer before His crucifixion, His prayer to His Father for you and for me, seemed to come alive and envelop the whole Theater as the complete seventeenth chapter of St. John was read: "After Jesus said this, he looked toward heaven and prayed:

FATHER, THE TIME HAS COME. GLORIFY YOUR SON, THAT YOUR SON MAY GLORIFY YOU. FOR YOU GRANTED HIM AUTHORITY OVER ALL PEOPLE THAT HE MIGHT GIVE ETERNAL LIFE TO ALL THOSE YOU HAVE GIVEN HIM. NOW THIS IS ETERNAL LIFE: THAT THEY MAY KNOW YOU, THE ONLY TRUE GOD, AND JESUS CHRIST, WHOM YOU HAVE SENT. . . . I HAVE GIVEN THEM THE GLORY THAT YOU GAVE ME, THAT THEY MAY BE ONE AS WE ARE ONE: I IN THEM AND YOU IN ME. MAY THEY BE BROUGHT TO COMPLETE UNITY TO LET THE WORLD KNOW THAT YOU SENT ME AND HAVE LOVED THEM EVEN AS YOU HAVE LOVED ME. . . .

As the curtain closed, the handbell choir began to play the hymn by C. Austin Miles, "In the Garden," ushering in an atmosphere of majesty. After the handbell choir had played the song, the choir began to sing, and the organ and piano joined in.

The words were on large overhead screens, and as the choir continued singing, everyone in the Theater started singing along:

> AND THE VOICE I HEAR, FALLING ON MY EAR, THE SON OF
> GOD DISCLOSES. AND HE WALKS WITH ME, AND HE TALKS
> WITH ME, AND HE TELLS ME I AM HIS OWN; AND THE JOY WE
> SHARE AS WE TARRY THERE NONE OTHER HAS EVER KNOWN.

It was a glorious moment and set a tone of total participation.

After the song, in a simple prayer of dedication, we invited Jesus to join us and take over the summit.

To prepare to worship with women from more than three hundred and fifty different churches, and in celebration of our diversity, we were invited to turn around and say to the person behind us: "It doesn't matter to me how you pray."

God requires a clean heart before He answers our prayers, so our leader gave an "Invitation to Repentance." Individually, we confessed our sins and asked Christ to cleanse us, giving Him permission to do what He wanted to do in us.

After we concluded this most important preliminary—repentance—we all began to worship God through the wonderful gift of music. We harmoniously petitioned the Almighty: *Change my heart, O God . . . You are the Potter, I am the clay; mold me and make me, this is what I pray.* After appealing to God, we turned to praise: *Blessed be the name of the Lord . . . The name of the Lord is a strong tower, the righteous run into it and they are saved.* We continued with wave after wave of musical praise until we closed this time of praise with the affirmation from the hymn by Joseph Scriven and Charles Converse:

> WHAT A FRIEND WE HAVE IN JESUS, ALL OUR SINS AND
> GRIEF TO BEAR! WHAT A PRIVILEGE TO CARRY EVERYTHING
> TO GOD IN PRAYER! OH, WHAT PEACE WE OFTEN FORFEIT;
> OH, WHAT NEEDLESS PAIN WE BEAR, ALL BECAUSE WE DO
> NOT CARRY, EVERYTHING TO GOD IN PRAYER!

A fun "Get Acquainted" time followed. We wanted to find out how much we had in common and yet how varied we were. Many different categories were called out, and as the women heard a category to which they belonged, they jumped up and shouted, "Hallelujah." They found themselves quickly jumping up, sitting down, and jumping up again and again, until every person in the Theater had been recognized in some way. Total participation continued to help everyone to feel a part of the whole.

A PERSONAL LETTER TO THE WOMEN

After all this fun, the mood quickly changed as Beverly Caesar, one of our committee members, began to read a personal letter to the women. She had been praying about what the Lord wanted her to say. One morning she was awakened very early and felt the Holy Spirit nudging her to "get up," although she was still tired and didn't feel like it. As she began to commune with the Lord at six o'clock on the morning of September

19, 1997, this letter, inspired by Psalm 139, came into her mind, and she immediately wrote it down.

I see beneath the cover-up, the makeup, and the dress-up. I am not looking at the color of your skin or the color of your hair. I see beneath the smile and beneath the frown. I do not see the length of your skirt or the clothing you wear. I see beyond your height, your size, your weight, and your gait.

I see a woman who has loved, who has given, who has shared, who has prayed. I see you at home, at work, and at church. I see you in your nakedness and in your shame. I see beyond the position you hold on your job or the lack of a job.

Today, I look beyond your college degree, your pedigrees, and your name. Today, I look beyond your titles of Reverend, Minister, Missionary, Evangelist, or Teacher. Today, I am going beyond your superb accomplishments, your acquisitions, and your plans.

*I see a woman living in the past, afraid of the future, afraid to love, afraid to care, afraid . . . afraid. I see a woman who has experienced pains at home, pains on the job, and pains in church. Your life pains have overwhelmed you, and you have masked it well, but today, **I see you.***

Today, I see beyond your singleness, your marriage, your desire to be married, your separation, and your divorce.

Today is your day of unmasking as you have come into the garden to spend time with Me. Today is your day of disrobing before hundreds of your sisters who are also gathered in the garden. Today is your day to come out of the cocoon that has restricted and bound you. The cocoons of guilt, grief, jealousy, unworthiness, shame, low self-esteem, pride, abuse, embar-

rassment, hatred, and an unforgiving spirit. You feel unfulfilled and unac-
complished, unloving and unloved, doubting and faithless.

I have been trying to get your attention for a very long time, but something or someone has kept you far away. Your schedule has not included Me
. . . I am always an afterthought. Your time is far spent doing something
else. I have diligently sought after you, and TODAY you have responded.

Some of you feel you have done enough. You are comfortable in the position where you sit. You are self-assured in your spiritual state. But today, I
have come to stand you up and show you another place. Remember, I can
see deep into your soul. I see a woman whom I loved, loved enough to obey
My Father and say, "Nevertheless, not My will, but Thine."

"Nevertheless" took me to Calvary, just for you. A willing "nevertheless" that made Me sacrifice My life for you—a love not to be compared
with any other.

Today is your Day of Jubilee. I will show you yourself. I will expose
you through My Word. Today, as we share in the garden, I will uncover
the you that your sisters think they know and expose the true woman
who lies behind the veils. Today is your day of release. I will set you free.
You will break through from the shackles and fly into a spiritual world
that I have appointed just for you.

Today, as we spend time in the garden talking and sharing, I will unlock
the joy that has been bound up in your soul . . . you will be set free. Free
from the guilt, the grief, the jealousy, the unworthiness, the shame, the low
self-esteem, the pride, the abuse, the embarrassment, the hatred, and the
unforgiving spirit. Today, you will be free to soar above the circumstances
of life that have kept you down.

Today, My beauty will be seen in you. You will come forth as a beau-

tiful flower with the aroma of praise; a beautiful flower with the grace of peace; a beautiful flower with the joy of thanksgiving; a beautiful flower with the poise of gentleness. A beautiful flower for the world to see, so they will know who I am and come to believe in Me.

Today, as we talk like never before, you will listen and follow My ways. Today, you and I will conquer the enemy of your soul and put him under your feet, because today is your Day of Jubilee.

Rejoice and clap your hands for the joy that fills your soul.

Rejoice and praise My Name, for the victory has come, and the battle has been won.

Rejoice and lift Me up, for today I have filled your cup.

Rejoice! Rejoice! Rejoice!

A beautiful contralto voice immediately filled the arena with two songs of exaltation to our Lord Jesus Christ.

THE THEATER BECOMES ABLAZE

The next speaker challenged each woman to be personally motivated to fast and pray for the transformation of her world and to be listening for what God wanted to do in and through her. The talk, "The Privilege and Power of Prayer," contended that if God brought the Women's Prayer Summit to pass as a result of one woman's prayer, what would He bring to pass as a result of all the combined prayers of thousands of women? Where would He take them in the future? How would He show His power in their lives? Each woman was charged to expand her knowledge of Christ through prayer. She was encouraged to ask God what He wanted to do through her. Audible voices of affirmation revealed their heightened expectations and eagerness to begin praying.

We sat forward in our seats, captivated with the interview of a young African-American sister, raised in a home with no father. She explained how Christ changed her and delivered her from a past of sexual promiscuity and guilt. She assured each woman that what Christ had done for her, He longed to do for everyone. Each person joined a group of three or four women to pray for all the women that this young woman represented, whether it was a daughter, sister, niece, friend, neighbor, a mother, or even oneself.

The Theater seemed to become ablaze with the thrill of communion with God. Each session of prayer was called to conclusion by the playing of instruments. It was always difficult to stop the session of prayer to continue on to the next interview.

The prayer intensity continued to build after an interview with a young Hispanic woman, who revealed her personal damage from a family history of dysfunction, including violence and murder. By God's grace and power, she had been delivered from the strongholds of drugs and prostitution and guilt from past abortions. God had given her a husband, a family, a home, and a local church in which they were all involved and where they found support.

This witness of God's grace and power was like a shot of faith-adrenalin to the women as they again went into prayers of intercession, boldly claiming: *For though we live in the world, we do not wage war as the world does. The weapons we fight with are not the weapons of the world. On the contrary, they have divine power to demolish strongholds. We demolish arguments and every pretension that sets itself up against the knowledge of God, and we take captive every thought to make it obedient to Christ* (2 Corinthians 10:3–5).

A young composer and pianist sang her own compositions, many of the words taken from Scripture, "Marvelous" and "Rend Your Heart." Raised hands, rocking, and crying revealed the emotional impact these songs had on the listeners.

The momentum kept building for the next simple but dynamic drama that addressed racial reconciliation. A non-threatening, noncondemning skit of four different ethnic and racial women very simply revealed their inner wounds from discrimination. The conclusion gave clear solutions from Scripture and personal experiences. The effect of the skit struck home as arrows of conviction hitting the bull's-eye of a target, becoming a prelude for three more women to expose their inner feelings regarding personal encounters of discrimination. In order that our Lord's Prayer for unity could be answered, all the walls of protection we had built around ourselves had to be breached. The walls of racial division were not the only barriers in the Theater that day.

One Hispanic woman told of how isolated and alienated she had felt when the kids laughed at her foreign accent. A Korean woman read a letter to an African-American woman with whom

she had worked many years before. In it, she apologized for being unkind and unloving simply because she didn't understand her. She asked for forgiveness. A Caucasian and an African-American woman spoke words of repentance and forgiveness and prayed for oneness and reconciliation. Their words of repentance and forgiveness were made personal by all the women as we sang the song written by Dick and Melodie Tunney, "Sisters."

> WE ARE SISTERS, SISTERS IN THE LORD; OUR FAITH IN COMMON, SISTERS IN THE LORD, NO MATTER HOW THE WORLD DEFINES US, NOTHING CAN BREAK THE TIE THAT BINDS US; WE ARE SISTERS IN THE LORD.

After an opportunity to make reconciliation personal, the afternoon portion of the Women's Prayer Summit closed at 5:00 P.M. It had been such an emotional and significant time for many of the women that as the time for dinner dismissal came, many did not leave the Theater. They did not want to break the spirit of what God was speaking into their lives.

Three hours had flown by, and we could hardly wait for the evening session to begin at 6:30 P.M.

TOUCHED BY HIS SPIRIT

The evening session began with music led by combined Spanish choirs in their own language. A Korean choir and a soloist followed with "How Great Thou Art" in their native tongue. No one could hold back, so we all began to sing together, with the languages mixed . . . "heavenly music"! Our praise continued as we sang "O the Glory of Your Presence" and the theme song specifically composed for the summit, "Touch Us with Your Spirit." He did!

Between the songs, an offering was taken. Afterward, as we were singing, one of our lawyers snuck up behind me and whispered that I should come to the "room." The "room" was where the ushers brought the offering. We had stationed a security officer at the door. As I opened the door, I gasped! I was speechless! The floor was covered inches deep with mostly one and five dollar bills! The offering baskets had overflowed, and the women were trying to count the money. I was so thankful that even though we had never anticipated such a bountiful offering, we had made preparations through our lawyer for it to be taken to a vault with a security officer.

As I returned to my seat, I praised God. I thought of all the women who had purchased a ticket in anticipation of meeting with Him and other believers. He had touched them with His Spirit, and they had responded with a tangible offering. This was one way they could express their enormous gratitude.

More interviews of our sisters shared the redeeming power of Christ in lives once devastated by sin. Wave after wave of powerful prayers targeted specific needs. We prayed for our spiritual, physical, psychological, and economic needs as women, and for the needs of our families, our city, our government, our churches, and our pastors. We prayed for protection from the evils rampant in the city. We prayed for our children—for their spiritual, physical, intellectual, and emotional protection. No facet of society was overlooked during this prayer time.

A sister who had returned from traveling the world prayed

(her story is in Chapter Eleven). Many in the Theater were brought to tears during her prayer for our persecuted sisters and their families all over the world. Detailed specifics of their unimaginable suffering—the loss of educational opportunities, jobs, homes, the jailing of believers, and even death for their faith—opened our eyes to what believers in Christ in some parts of the world endure for their faith. Her prayer included other needs of the great majority of poor in the world, particularly about the effects of human bondage, trafficking of children and young women, the sale of children into prostitution, the sale of women, poverty, abandonment, and homelessness.

HOSANNA IN THE HIGHEST

The blare of a shofar introduced a Jewish sister who had discovered Messiah while attending high school in California. She gave a clear picture of salvation and shared how she came to believe that Jesus was the Promised One sent from God. He lived a life without sin and paid the penalty of sin for every man, woman, and child by dying on the cross. He defeated death and Satan when He rose from the sealed grave on the third day. He is now seated at the right hand of the Father and says, "Whosoever will may come." Messiah had become her Savior when she confessed her sins, gave Him her life, and asked Him to be her Redeemer.

Just when we thought we could get no higher, we were catapulted further upward with the reminder, "There Is a Redeemer," from a professional opera soloist. The sound filled every corner of the room, and many women rose in unison with arms outstretched.

With God's presence filling the Theater, two important events remained before the evening's closing. First, an invitation to enter the Savior's garden by accepting the salvation of Christ was extended, followed by a special communion service.

As the same vocalist, accompanied by the handbell choir, began to sing "We Shall Behold Him" and followed it with F. E. Weatherly's "The Holy City," it seemed that Jesus was so close that if we reached up we would surely grasp His hand. She proclaimed:

LAST NIGHT I LAY A-SLEEPING, THERE CAME A DREAM SO FAIR, I STOOD IN OLD JERUSALEM, BESIDE THE TEMPLE THERE. I HEARD THE CHILDREN SINGING, AND EVER AS THEY SANG, METHOUGHT THE VOICE OF ANGELS FROM HEAV'N IN ANSWER RANG . . . JERUSALEM, JERUSALEM, LIFT UP YOUR GATES AND SING; HOSANNA IN THE HIGHEST, HOSANNA TO YOUR KING.

AND THEN METHOUGHT THE DREAM HAD CHANGED, THE STREETS NO LONGER RANG. BUT WITH A GLAD HOSANNA THE LITTLE CHILDREN SANG. THE SUN GREW DARK WITH MYSTERY, THE MORN WAS COLD AND CHILL, BUT THE SHADOW OF A CROSS AROSE UPON A LONELY HILL . . . JERUSALEM, JERUSALEM, HARK, HOW THE ANGELS SING; HOSANNA THROUGH THE AGES, HOSANNA TO YOUR KING!

THEN ONCE AGAIN THE SCENE WAS CHANGED, NEW EARTH THERE SEEMED TO BE. I SAW THE HOLY CITY BESIDE THE TIMELESS SEA. THE LIGHT OF GOD WAS ON ITS STREETS, THE GATES WERE OPEN WIDE; AND ALL WHO WOULD MIGHT

ENTER AND NO ONE WAS DENIED. NO NEED OF MOON OR
STARS BY NIGHT OR SUN TO SHINE BY DAY, IT WAS THE
NEW JERUSALEM THAT WOULD NOT PASS AWAY. IT WAS
THE NEW JERUSALEM THAT WOULD NOT PASS AWAY.
JERUSALEM, JERUSALEM, SING FOR THE NIGHT IS O'ER;
HOSANNA IN THE HIGHEST, HOSANNA FOR EVER MORE.
HOSANNA IN THE HIGHEST, HOSANNA FOR EVER MORE.

Promptly at 9:00 P.M., the Women's Prayer Summit closed
with a praise and dismissal prayer. As the curtain closed, the
women did not want to leave.

A security guard stood at the base of the stage. After the close
of the program, a recently widowed sister-in-law of one of our
Executive Committee members saw tears in the guard's eyes and
approached him. He asked her what he needed to do to become
a Christian. She led him to Jesus and salvation. He later attended their church in Jamaica, Queens, New York.

We were thrilled that at the end of the night the venue manager told us that we were the most well-organized "religious
group" the Garden had ever experienced. We praised God!

As I was leaving, I spotted two groups of women from the
prayer summit standing outside of Madison Square Garden talking to passersby. In one of the groups, a man was praying to
accept Jesus as his Lord!

An awesome aura of the Lord's presence, drawing power, and
glory enveloped the summit. It descended upon the women, and
as they departed, it accompanied them. It even seemed to rest
upon the building itself. The Holy Spirit was almost irresistible

in the most nonintrusive manner one could imagine. It was equal to what I had sensed on my knees in prayer two years earlier, when the Lord gave the vision on August 20, 1995.

I drove home exhausted but filled with gratitude and praise for the Lord's mercy. He had surely manifested His pleasure in this assembly.

A HARVEST REVEALED

The following morning began to reveal an inkling of what had taken place in individual lives at the summit. As each of our Executive Committee members attended their individual churches for Sunday worship, woman after woman reported their experiences at the summit. At one of the churches, a congressman was a visiting speaker for that morning. He talked about his wife's report from attending the summit and went on to state: "This is the answer for New York City." As I entered my own church, several young women rushed to tell me of how God had touched them at the prayer summit. All I could do was bow my knees in thanksgiving to God for meeting all of us with such an incredible force.

The following Monday morning a New York City Christian Radio DJ, the late Andy Anderson, called for an interview to talk about what had transpired on Saturday. As we talked, he opened the mikes and invited women who had attended the prayer summit to call in. This was an unannounced opportunity, but women from all over the metropolitan New York City area called and told of what God had done in their hearts and minds at the prayer summit.

Several young college women told me personally of how encouraging it was to have Christian women as visible role models. They talked about how hard it was to stand firm in their faith. In their college classes, they had women professors who ridiculed their Christian faith and their views on moral issues. Some of these young women were first-generation citizens and came from family backgrounds where their mothers were unprepared to help them.

My only daughter described her thrilling experience on the back row with my precious five-week-old grandson. At the beginning of the program, she, her baby, and a group of African-American women were sitting together. Off to the side was a lone white woman, obviously separated from them. During the skit about our differences, the testimonies about racial and cultural alienation, and the subsequent time of prayer, the walls began to come down. By the end of the evening, they were together—all as one.

A program was handed to every woman entering the theater with a questionnaire inserted in the middle. Over twelve hundred women took the time to fill them out and return them to the ushers. We were astonished when we discovered only two negative responses. Unbelievable! One question asked what we could do to improve the summit, and we loved the comment, *"Nothing. Only the Second Coming of Jesus could have improved it."* We also received some very helpful comments as to how the next summit could be improved.

The most surprising and thrilling fact we discovered was that more than three hundred women recorded that they had asked Jesus to be their personal Lord. The Executive Committee had incorrectly assumed that only believing women would give up a Saturday, go to the expense of coming into the city, and, in addition, "pay to pray." Consequently, we had no plans as to how to handle these many new believers. Our Executive Committee member, who covered the borough of Queens, quickly organized volunteers to phone, counsel, and pray with every woman who had placed her life in the hands of Jesus. If she had no church affiliation, the name and address of a church home where she could worship and continue her spiritual growth was suggested.

One church from Harlem had reserved a bus to take members to the summit, but it never came. At the last minute, they hopped on public transportation. On the way home, their public transportation cars were filled with women who had attended the summit. They were singing together, and some were quietly talking to other passengers about Jesus and how He could bring new life to them. They reported that they had never experienced such a blessed public transportation ride. They were so thankful the bus had never shown up.

ON A PERSONAL NOTE

Can you imagine my thrill when my daughter, several years later, told me, "I have attended other inspiring events where many thousands of women gathered, and they were lots of fun, but I left the same as I had come. When I attended the Women's Prayer Summit, I came one person but I left another person. I was forever changed as a result of that day." Could any mother ever ask for anything greater?

How did this wonderful opportunity ever come to me, a most improbable woman? How was I allowed the privilege of knowing my faith sisters of color and culture, many of them very different from me? How did I have the thrill of working so closely with them, to see life through their eyes and experiences, to feel God's gift of love for them grow within my heart to inexpressible proportions, to learn from these great women of faith, and to see God work miracle after miracle as He opened hearts and doors to bring about this prayer summit, to see my faith become reality for others to see?

All these and countless experiences were mine, I was reminded, because I had discovered the closet of private prayer. PRAYER! That's where God gives the seed that grows to produce the harvest.

CHAPTER TWO

The Seeds That
Produce the Harvest

(JANET BROLING)

We should not pray for

greater works,

prayer is the greater work.

—Oswald Chambers

The call awakened me very early, Sunday morning, August 20, 1995. I could not go back to sleep. As I lay in the quiet darkness, I sensed the displeasure of my Lord. I was troubled by something I had done that weekend. His gentle nudging continued, so I slipped out of bed and crept downstairs to my private place of prayer. I needed to solve this problem with my Lord (to make it right), so that my fellowship with Him could be quickly restored.

"Sin!" Why do we resist calling it what it is? Why is it so hard to admit?

I knew that I had sinned, so I confessed it. God's forgiveness washed over my soul as peace pushed away my troubled spirit. I found myself praising Him that my salvation did not depend upon my good works, but upon Christ's complete payment of my sin when He died upon the cross.

As I was kneeling in prayer, a surprising call for action came. An image flashed into my mind . . . a large assembly of people, but something was different. This assembly was filled with the presence of God! It defied description! It was so graphic, in a place so specific, Madison Square Garden, that I wrote it down; but not before I cried out, "Not there, Lord. That is too big. The acoustics are not good." (I had been in Madison Square Garden only once for a tennis match.) I feared that the impression would fade, so I wrote as fast as I could: "Focus—*Jesus*. No big names to attract crowds, only *Jesus*. No remuneration for anyone—this will be a sacrifice of love to our Lord."

I long had desired to see the Name of *Jesus* on a secular marquee in New York City. I wanted all who drove or walked by to realize that there were many people in this great city with a strong faith in Him and in His Lordship over every aspect of their lives, even their entertainment.

With this early morning encounter, God began to water and nurture my long embedded desire. An explosion of energy surged through my body and mind. I had an immediate burning desire to bring this about. I also sensed that if I didn't respond and act upon this, someone else would get the assignment, and I did not want to miss out.

Simultaneous with the tremendous exhilaration of doing something new, something I had never done before, I also understood the need for caution. Scripture tells us to *test the spirits to see if they are from God* (1 John 4:1). I determined to proceed with care. After I finished praying and writing, I went back to bed and slept until it was time to get up for church.

The next morning I awakened with sustained energy and excitement. The events on Sunday had continued to strengthen and confirm the mental picture I had while praying earlier that morning. It surpassed anything I had ever experienced!

During prayer on Monday, I said, "Lord, I will go forward. I will simply put one foot in front of the other, so long as You open the door. When You close the door, I will be freed from this vision and will go on with my life as normal."

I decided to find out if the first door was going to open or slam shut, so I headed for the telephone. The first step of exploration was so intimidating! My hand seemed to drop from the weight of the phone as I picked it up and called information for the telephone number of "The Madison Square Garden." As I waited for a response to my dialed number, the thump from my heartbeat seemed to be so loud that I wondered if it could be heard at the other end of the line. I pondered, *Will the venue be available? Will they lease it to me? Or will the door be closed now?*

A delightful young man answered the phone. I told him what I had in mind and asked if the venue was available? To my great surprise, it was, and he added: "Come on down." It was as if God was allowing rain to fall upon the seed that I was certain He had planted in my mind. I was told that I needed ONLY to bring a deposit and sign the contract—that became the under-statement of the year! (It would be many months and lawyer's conferences before we actually signed the contract.) I made an appointment for the following Monday morning to begin the process. This would give seven days of exploratory time—time for the Son to shine upon the seed.

I had barely hung up the phone when I found my fingers punching the phone number of a mentor and prayer partner. I asked if I might come to her house to pray. I decided to seek the counsel of one of the wisest believers I knew. Upon my arrival and after listening, she prayed, "Lord, if this is from You, will You please open a door that no man can close? But if it is not from You, will You please close a door that no man can open?" A great sense of peace swept over me as she prayed. She inquired as to my next step.

I needed my husband's blessing. If he objected, the door would be closed—period. After dinner that evening, as I shared the vision with him, he responded, "Well, if you think the Lord is calling you to do this, you had better do it." However, his body language told me that he felt I might have "gone around the corner" on this one.

DAYS OF PRAYER AND FASTING

Tuesday, as I awakened, the energy and peace I had experienced since early Sunday morning were replaced with panic, doubt, and even *fear*. I thought to myself, *Who do I think I am to try to do something like this?* But then I reflected upon Jesus—upon the great I AM—and I concluded that if this idea was coming from Him, it was no big deal. The important question was: Is the vision from God?

Sallie Vroom has wisely said, "Whether God reveals something small or something extraordinary, we must learn to discern His voice. If the task is large, an obstacle—panic [a weed!]—may set in if we are not sure that God is leading us."

I found myself asking, "Is Jesus really speaking to me through His Holy Spirit? How do I know it is not MY idea? How will I know it is the voice of the Holy Spirit?"

I discovered an unsettling sense of uncertainty. I even hesitated to acknowledge it. This vision was consistent with the way God had spoken to me in the past, but its scope was so much larger than any previous experience that I felt a new fear. If the doors were closed on this, and I had misread the leading of the Lord, would I ever again be confident to step out in faith to follow what I felt was His leading? Conversely, I did not want to be guilty of presumption.

The following prayer expressed my inner struggle:

Oh, Lord God, I believe. Help my unbelief! I know nothing is too hard for You. As I face the possibility that You are leading me to do something that I have never done before, I am filled with excitement.

Yet, Lord, I am keenly aware of who I am—of my limitations. I have never walked this path before.

Have I heard You correctly? I am afraid to trust my own perceptions. I know that You lead us from faith to faith. I ask that You purify my desire.

If I may be assured that this vision is from You, then I know You will not only cover my back but that You will also walk before me to open doors and hearts so this assembly may become a reality to bring glory to You.

May I have the assurance that I am moving in obedience to You and only You? In the precious Name of Jesus, I humbly, with thanksgiving, pray. Amen.

I determined to spend three days fasting, praying, and seeking additional counsel. Scripture advises: *I will praise the LORD who counsels me; even at night my heart instructs me* (Psalm 16:7) and that *there is wisdom in many counselors* (Proverbs 15:22).

My husband was leaving on a fishing trip the following day, and my plans had been made weeks earlier to visit a friend in Pennsylvania. When I arrived at her home, I shared the story, and she joined the last day of my fast.

The weekend visit gave us a lot of time for brainstorming and prayer. We discussed the difficulty of getting women from the suburbs into the city for such an assembly. She asked, "How are you going to fill that place with women?" I replied, "I have absolutely no idea how *the Lord* is going to fill that place."

I did not know where to begin. Here I was, looking at the largest metropolitan area in the country, to do something that had never been done before. I knew only two Christian women in Manhattan and no pastors. How would I, an unknown fifty-eight-year-old woman, reach pastors? Even if I was able to contact them, why would they listen to a no-name layperson? (Public relations experts later informed me that the larger the city, the more difficult it is to reach and gather individuals. Fortunately, I was not yet aware of that fact.)

How could I challenge and motivate pastors to encourage the women of their churches to assemble in a secular venue and pay to pray, when they could pray for free at their home churches? Would they recognize any benefit for their congregations—for them? Would they suspect I had a hidden agenda? Would they think I was *crazy*? How would the women respond, especially when they heard they were being asked to volunteer their time, energy, and talents, and to swallow their egos and headline Jesus? The obstacles loomed upward and would grow to appear mountainous!

Frankly, from all appearances, God could have picked no more unlikely a person for this task. Obviously, the method of operation for this assignment would be: *Not by might nor by power, but by my Spirit, says the LORD Almighty* (Zechariah 4:6).

The late Dr. Bill Bright's first book on fasting and prayer was new on the market. A prayer partner had read it and insisted there must be fasting and prayer coverage for the vision. A member of her Bible study organized a group of women from six states to conduct a forty-day rotational fasting and praying schedule. From October 1 through November 9, 1995, a minimum of two women fasted from midnight to midnight each day of the week. They asked God to direct and order every facet of the proposed assembly. The seed began to show immediate life!

In the middle of the fasting period, six of the women came to New Jersey for a day and night of specific fasting and prayer. Together, we brought every aspect of the assembly before Christ and asked what He wanted. We prayed about the venue itself, the actual date, the name, the participants, the program, and every detail we could imagine.

Several of these women sensed a great harvest and even thought that the name of the assembly should include the word *harvest*. I, at that time, did not see a "harvest," because I had always associated harvest with evangelism and preaching. After the prayer summit, I realized it is *prayer that brings the harvest.*

DOORS BEGIN TO OPEN

In response to the praying women, God immediately began to open doors amazingly. I experienced the power of networking. Friends called friends. Again and again, as I followed up with a phone call, I found ministry leaders not only in town, but answering their own phones. Each door I pushed seemed to open. So I simply continued to walk through them.

Complications, however, accompanied the open doors. A lawyer friend advised that a public relations expert was imperative. But how would I find an expert with such a heart of devotion to Jesus that she would consider it a privilege to donate her time and abilities? The volunteering of time and talent as a sacrifice of love to Jesus was a vital part of the call of the assembly. These challenges loomed as a giant wall.

I frequently awakened in the middle of the night thinking about all the hurdles to be overcome to bring about such an assembly. Often unable to go back to sleep, I found myself downstairs praying.

On one of those very early mornings, the Lord gave me this special poem. It became my poem of faith as I often prayed it back to Him.

> *I will praise You, O my God,*
>   *You are wonderful indeed*
> *I will watch to see Your hand*
>   *as You solve our every need*
> *You will answer when we call*
>   *and Your vision we will heed*
> *Though details loom as a wall*
>   *Your right hand will make them fall*
> *We will watch Your mighty power*
>   *as You bring Your faithful throng*
> *All the women of our land*
>   *Praising You in verse and song*
> *You will wash away our sin*
>   *as we call upon Your name*
> *Shattered lives will be made whole*
>   *through the blood of Christ our lamb*
> *You will heal our broken souls*
>   *and restore our fractured homes*
> *Bringing praise from every lip*
>   *to the One who conquered death*

Are you ready for a miracle? In December 1995, I called an acquaintance in New York City. We originally met on an airplane as seat partners. It had been one of those *divine* appointments. This day, as we talked, she asked what she could do. I told her of our immediate need of a public relations director and nearly fell off my chair with her response, "I know exactly the woman for you." I could hardly believe what I was hearing as she rattled off all the qualifications of a friend who had been very successful in public relations for a television network on the West Coast and was presently living in New York City.

I immediately called this young professional and met with her and her husband. A few days later, when she said yes, I could hardly keep from shouting into the phone! God was opening *doors* in the greater metropolitan New York area in response to the prayers of His women. It was awesome. This is how God began to do the impossible—impossible for me, but not for the Creator of the universe.

In January 1996, I felt the leading of the Holy Spirit to call Dr. McKenzie Pier, founder of Concerts of Prayer in greater New York City. Mac didn't know me at that time, although we had a mutual friend, Barbara Boyd, who had served as spiritual mentor to both of us and to mutual acquaintances. For years Mac had been working to bring churches and pastors together for prayer in the Name of Jesus. As Mac and I met, talked, and prayed, we agreed that by working together we could bring glory to our Lord and His church. Concerts of Prayer provided contacts with ministry leaders and pastors all over the metropolitan New York City area. I believe it was only the Lord who prompted him to take such a risk and step out in faith to endorse the vision.

SHARING THE VISION

Our new public relations director, Joni, decided the best way to reach the pastors, share the vision, receive their input, and answer any questions was to host strategically located focus groups. She worked closely with Concerts of Prayer and their public relations director, Beverly, to set up our first focus group in Flushing Queens, New York.

I will never forget the experience as we stepped out of the car to enter our first focus group. The Lord's presence was so apparent. It was as if we were walking on holy ground. It was not one of our larger groups, but a significant and diverse group of pastors and women ministry leaders from Queens, Brooklyn, Long Island, and New Jersey were gathered.

The female attendees completely caught the vision and said, "Let's go." Some of the pastors, however, were more reticent, perhaps due to their experience. They thought:

- Women would never pay to pray when they could pray at home or at church for free.
- Women would never come into the city without a big name to attract them.
- The timing of October 1997 was too soon. The earliest this could happen would be 1998.

After the focus group, one pastor said that as he was driving home, he had the feeling this was of God, but that it was an

"Ishmael." Since we did not want to take matters into our own hands, we decided to go back to prayer and research and wait until the pastors said, "Go."

We knew this gathering was of God, and we were determined it would be done God's way or not at all. We would not try to push our way in. It was vital that the local pastors be in agreement and give their blessing to any large women's gathering. This is also a biblical concept. The pastors are shepherds to their flocks. They are responsible to God for any spiritual input they endorse that enters the lives and minds of their flock.

While we were waiting for a "green light" from the pastors, we kept praying and working. We surveyed twelve national and international ministry leaders and asked them, "What grips the heart of the women in your ministry?" Their answers were helpful, and most answers were basically similar: women, married or single, wanted to feel they were making a significant contribution to the world by their lives. Married women and mothers were concerned about their marriages and their children.

One day during this waiting period, John, one of our personal pastors of many years before, called to see how things were going. Soon after I told him we were waiting for the pastors' "green light," I received the following handwritten note:

8/1/96

Dear Janet,

You did not ask my opinion, but we're close enough to give it any way—Move w/o the pastors. It's a woman VISION, women thing. God spoke to women—not the pastors. Church history is full of accounts of things happening when women pray. Pastors are always too busy—often an excuse. I think God spoke to you. Nehemiah had plenty of detractors, he pressed on. If the pastors are detractors, pray for them, move forward w/ the vision, and pray for them when Madison Square Garden is filled w/women praying.

This busy pastor had written this enormously encouraging note while on an airplane. It was as if God had reached down, taken his hand, and written this personal note to me. It came at such a crucial time that I saved it. That letter was a personal affirmation that the pastors' blessing would eventually be given.

October 1996 became decision time. We needed a specific answer as to whether we would gain the blessing of the pastors. Without it we would consider this a closed door from the Lord, and I would go on with my life as normal. We organized seven more focus groups. The schedule was a grueling one with six groups in three days.

This may not sound like such an arduous task unless one has lived in the metropolitan New York area and tried to drive from borough to borough and state to state. It can be exhausting. The other drivers can be downright menacing, and, to make it more challenging, I was unfamiliar with most of these areas. A normal commute of thirty minutes could take up to an hour and a half or even two hours. The flow of the traffic ruled.

At our second focus group, as I was crossing the George Washington Bridge, my never-friendly-fellow-drivers refused to let me squeeze into the exit lane, so I missed my exit! I eventually found myself sitting in front of a rather suspicious-looking auto repair shop in the Bronx not far from Yankee Stadium. With no idea of how to get back to the bridge, I just sat and prayed. Then I looked up and watched a man come out the front door of the shop. He swung up behind the wheel of a white panel truck parked in front of me. I waited until his door was closed, then pulled up even with him. I rolled down my window partway and said, "I missed my exit into Manhattan and need to get back to the bridge." "Follow me," he shouted. I soon found myself back on the correct route to my destination. However, from the pace of my heartbeats, it is probably safe to assume my blood pressure was elevated! God's provisions in small details never ceased to amaze me.

The focus groups brought many surprises. God taught us so much through them. At a Long Island focus group, a Christian newspaper editor said, "As I listen to this, I'm reminded of Joshua. He marched around the city of Jericho for six days, and on the seventh day the walls fell down." On the way home, Joni said, "We need six mini-prayer summits in the spring of 1997 to get ready for the October assembly in Madison Square Garden." After I gasped and then caught my breath, I had to agree, even though they had not been in our plan.

After the last focus group in Manhattan, a young woman called and identified herself as a lawyer. She worked for a large prestigious Manhattan law firm. My faith had been increasing daily by the doors God was opening, but I knew God was pulling out the stops when she said, "What can I do?" I tried to remain calm and said, "We need a lawyer." I explained to her that the individual who had helped us was becoming so busy he was unable to continue, and we needed a good lawyer to keep us out of trouble. The complex venue contract carried penalties of $25,000 for "each and every" violation—a misspelled name or any unapproved promotion could trigger it. We were also in a state where incorporation for non-profit religious groups was rigorous.

She promised to ask one of the partners of her firm if they would sponsor a pro bono arrangement. The answer was yes! Their firm would handle all of our legal needs with no payment expected. God was at it again! The seeds were not only sprouting, they were shooting up! To more fully describe this miracle, at the end of our first fiscal year, this law firm had given us the equivalent of $110,000 in *free* legal fees. They took care of our New York State non-profit incorporation, our contract, budget and financial figures, annual meetings, insurance contracts, arbitration agreements, etc.

Our legal meetings were held in an elegant, cherry-paneled, corner conference room overlooking Lexington Avenue. We were seated around a huge mahogany conference table complete with food and soft drinks, as if we were one of their important paying clients. We were blessed with the most competent legal care available. It was something that only God could do!

OUR VISION, OUR CALL FROM THE LORD!

To this point, our prayer team remained the original group of women from six states. At each focus group, evaluation sheets were distributed and then gathered at the end of the meeting. After the completion of all the focus groups, we combined their evaluation sheets with the ministry survey results gathered from national and international ministry leaders. We sent them to our prayer team and to our four Executive Committee members. After a period of prayer and study of all the surveys, everyone agreed that the name should be the *Women's Prayer Summit* and the prayer summit would be held in October 1997. It had been fourteen months since the August 1995 vision until this decision in October 1996.

Our Lord had multiplied the seed from a prayer journal entry to an Executive Committee of four women (three more would soon be added), a prayer team, a legal team, and two public relations experts (though we would soon lose one of them).

At each focus group, there had been women who seemed to stand out as potential Executive Committee members. We approached these women and asked them to join our Executive Committee. Before the focus groups began, we knew Concert of Prayer's public relations director, Beverly, would be one of these women. She was a faith missionary and would split her time between Concerts of Prayer and us. There were other women we would have loved to join our committee, but their schedules made it impossible. Some of them joined our Advisory Board.

On December 11, 1996, I received a call from Joni with bittersweet news. She was pregnant with their second child. Her first pregnancy was difficult, and this pregnancy would require a lot of rest. I was delighted for her and her husband, but I felt a tremendous personal loss. I had depended upon her, and I didn't know how the void could be filled. The Lord had to remind me that I was to depend upon Him. He had orchestrated this assembly, and it would be fully staffed.

We still lacked our critical endorsement—the pastors' blessing—which came in January 1997 at the annual Pastors' Prayer Summit, where several hundred pastors from different denominations, ages, ethnicities, and styles of worship gathered in the Name of Jesus to pray for revival and renewal. We were invited by Concerts of Prayer to attend and share the vision. To my amazement, the pastor who led the pastors' prayer of blessing upon us was the same man who, after our first focus group, had said the idea of a prayer summit seemed like an "Ishmael."

Another event at that Pastors' Prayer Summit confirmed God's continual encouragement to me personally. Earlier, at one of our focus groups, after I had shared the vision of this assembly, one of the pastors had jokingly asked, "Are you sure you didn't eat something spicy the night before?" Though I had laughed, the remark had stung. It made me wonder if he really believed that the idea was of God. After a session of prayer at the Pastors' Prayer Summit, this same pastor walked across the room to where I was sitting, put his hand upon my head, and said, "Rise up, O woman of God." I have no idea if he remembered his remark at the focus group, but I remembered it. God was so gracious to answer my concern.

The first decision of our newly formed Executive Committee settled the date, October 4, 1997, in The Theater At Madison Square Garden. Three of our executive members were not yet with us, but four of us went to the venue, prayed, and had peace with our decision.

The signing of the contract was the first big step of faith that our Executive Committee took together. The Women's Prayer Summit was no longer my vision; it was now our vision! Together, we would follow our Lord's leading. We had a huge contract to fulfill. The real work was about to begin, and we had only eight months!

We immediately needed literature and advertising, worthy in appearance to represent our Lord, and a clarion call that would compel busy women to join with us and attend.

Again, God supplied! A good friend of mine recommended her close friend Sallie. She had worked in advertising and marketing for many years, and she volunteered her talent and ability. This was her gift of love to Jesus and to His Kingdom. Her creativity and ability produced beautiful brochures, stationery, and every piece of literature we required. These needed to be completed before we began our meetings.

God never stopped providing counsel. Another friend had recommended that I call Dr. Robert Bakke. In an unscheduled telephone call to his office, he had generously shared the following wisdom: "If you plan it and ask them to come, they won't come. Make them part of the planning, and they will take ownership." He also counseled of the importance of a clarion call. It must be so clear to the women that it would overcome the fear of going into the city at night, be worth the ticket price, child care, the expense of travel, and take precedence over the responsibilities and pleasures normally performed on a Saturday. We had to reach the women of this metropolitan New York City area, and they had to be assured that this prayer summit would be something they would not want to miss.

Sallie came up with our clarion call, *Come to the Garden*.

MINI-PRAYER SUMMITS PAVE THE WAY

Before we began this phase, our last three Executive Committee members came on board. I once heard the statement: *God is seldom early, but never late.* That is how I felt with the completion of our Executive Committee. Oh, how we needed them.

Our original fasting prayer team from six states carried the prayer responsibility of the Women's Prayer Summit until our new chairman joined the committee in January. She brought a network of women dedicated to the power of prayer and greatly expanded it throughout the city.

We planned that all our introductory meetings should be held between early February and May 30. After June 1, we would devote the summer to prayer and preparation for the October 4 Women's Prayer Summit in The Theater At Madison Square Garden.

Our six mini-prayer summits were held on Saturday mornings from 9:30 until 11:30. Each mini-prayer summit required a host church that would recruit other surrounding churches to join with them. Thousands of letters of invitation and brochures were mailed to individuals and churches. Everyone worked to get the word out to as many women as possible. Radio interviews, Christian newspapers, and magazine articles also helped. In addition to the mini-prayer summits, we had eleven meetings for women ministry leaders. Most of them were also held on Saturdays.

As we began the mini-prayer summits, we began to catch a glimpse of what God had in store for us. Women who would leave the security of their preferred church and denomination, their comfortable form of worship and music, to join with other sisters in Christ found a great blessing. They discovered an understanding of one another as they listened to three women interviewed at each mini-prayer summit. In the interviews, we learned our sisters had lived through indescribable sorrows and rejections by their own families and others. Rebellion in youth had led some into drugs, uncontrolled sexual sins, pregnancies, abortions, and guilt—always guilt. The experiences varied—broken health, broken marriages, terminally ill children, death of children, and the resulting devastation and depression. Some had been imprisoned. Others had family members who were guilty of theft, murder, etc. In a city as large as New York City, as diverse as the United Nations itself, we learned the church is truly a shelter for the broken.

Often, we in suburbia and rural areas go to church, and everyone looks great on the exterior. People seldom feel free to share their true inner struggles with one another. Perhaps this is due to a fear of rejection, perhaps it is our culture, or perhaps we do not want to know the problems of the person sitting by our side—for then we might have to become involved, and who has time for that?

In our mini-prayer summits, the Holy Spirit began to open our hearts as we all prayed as one in the Name of Jesus Christ. The diversity began to melt away, and a new empathy for one another replaced it.

All seven women of our Executive Committee attended and had a vital role in each of these meetings unless an emergency arose. In addition, they attended our regular Executive Committee meetings. This was a tremendously time-consuming responsibility for them. They all lived in different boroughs. Getting into the city for our meetings was difficult enough, but when we traveled to all these various locations for the mini-prayer summits and women ministry leaders' meetings, the difficulties intensified. The distances, traffic, tolls, child care expenses, and obstacles seemed never ending. In addition, all these women had other employment responsibilities. The responsibilities and details of such an event required seven organized women who truly gave sacrificially.

THE RUN TO THE FINISH LINE

By the first day of June, most of the preliminary meetings had been completed, and our focus shifted toward the Women's Prayer Summit as our strategic plan outlined. Our New York prayer network began to multiply. A prayer network with more than four hundred members devoted three months of their prayer letter to the requests of the summit. Many churches held special prayer times and days for this assembly. We all worked tirelessly, but we also knew that God was giving us added endurance and working on our behalves because of the prayers.

Advertising was placed in newspapers, journals, magazines, churches, through various ministries, and on radio. Thousands of brochures were distributed. The committee members were interviewed on Christian radio and one on Christian television. Each committee member also wrote and recorded six *minute prayers.* They aired on Christian radio in the metropolitan New York City area as "A Prayer Moment" for forty days prior to the October 4 gathering.

Ticketing was a whole other area of expertise. Two of our members organized ticket sales and attendance. They had hoards of women working with them.

As we headed into the planning of the actual program for October 4, we encountered severe spiritual warfare. Had we not been so covered by prayer, it is possible that conflict could have derailed all that God wanted to do. As we gathered to plan the program for the day, we experienced things we had never experienced before. Discoveries were revealed about one another that we did not like or could not, on our own, overlook and overcome. Disagreement surfaced that appeared to be very serious. (You will read more about this later.)

As the children of Israel had marched around Jericho for six days at the instruction of the Lord in preparation for the walls to tumble when the trumpets sounded, so the mini-prayer summits had paved the way for the walls of spiritual warfare to crumble. At our next Executive Committee meeting, the Holy Spirit brought sharing and an openness. A brokenness of individuals' spirits paved the way for a regeneration of God's love to give a servant's heart back to the committee members. Satan was defeated! The walls of separation were broken down, and love one for another rushed back. Only prayer can effect such changes in hearts (2 Corinthians 10:4)!

Our Prayer Chairman realized that we needed additional prayer covering. She organized another forty-day rotational fast planned to end on October 4. Everyone was invited to join with the Executive Committee to fast and pray for the Lord's Spirit to fall and break down the walls of disunity in our city and replace them with unity in the Name of Jesus. We have no idea how many actually joined us.

Details, details, details! Letters of invitations. Programs

designed and printed. Banners printed and fireproofed. Meetings with the venue. Sound people. A Project Manager for October 4 (to comply with our contract). Transportation. Buses. Church bulletin inserts. Communion packets. Attendance coordinators. Ticket sales. Outreach Chairman. More churches to contact. And on and on it continued.

The music presented a unique opportunity, but problems as well. Music had to be chosen and licenses obtained. Our music committee (not members of our Executive Committee) gathered a choir from all over the city. You can imagine the complications their practices presented. The location had to be central enough for all to get there after work. That was nearly impossible. There were soloists, instrumentalists, a praise group, and a bell choir to be assembled, practiced, and readied.

The Executive Committee now met weekly as we worked toward refining the program. A huge fine would be levied if we went one minute over the closing time. This required everyone participating in the program to work on the message God had given them. We timed everything and then scheduled it accordingly to avoid overtime charges. Only prayer could guide us to design a program that had to be so controlled and yet give the Holy Spirit freedom and time to work among us.

A Story That Must Be Told

By October 3, 1997, we were about to see the awesome power of the Holy Spirit reveal the presence of Jesus as He would fall upon The Theater At Madison Square Garden.

As I later reread my prayer journal for this day, I discovered something personal and very special. The penultimate detail of my day on October 3 was a trip to the airport to pick up our daughter and her two sons. Sam was four and a half, and Benjamin was five weeks old. At that time, they were our only grandchildren. As Ann came off the airplane, the baby was sound asleep. I carried him to the car in my arms as he continued to sleep. That was very unusual for him, as he was not a good sleeper. Late that night, as we made our way up the stairs to our bedrooms, Ann said, "Mom, you are so calm. Aren't you nervous?" I answered, "No, but I know why. I have been sustained by all the prayer that has surrounded this assembly. Christ has given me the ultimate assurance that this is His assembly."

One question often asked of any large evangelical event is, "Are the decisions made in such a setting only emotional and temporary, or are they truly life changing?"

Would reconciliation between the churches in the metropolitan New York City area be lasting or temporary? What about the racial and cultural unity that began at the summit? Would the friendships within the committee continue or fall apart?

Five years from the forming of our Executive Committee, I was invited back to New York to meet once again with all the women who had served on the two Executive Committees. It was the first time we had all been together in five years. As we met, we discovered that the bond among us was stronger than ever.

A public relations expert who attended said, "Normally, after five years of separation, relationships between people have diminished to the point where they have very little in common. *This story must be told.*"

Another question often asked about a large event is, "Is it worth all the expense, time, and energy it takes?" I must admit that I also asked that question.

One day in prayer, I heard the Lord whisper, "Write the story." I went back to New York to interview eight women who had served with me as Executive Committee members for the two Women's Prayer Summits. I also interviewed one of our original fasting and prayer partners. I wanted to learn what God had done in their lives as a result of the summit, and where He had taken them in the years since. It has now been almost ten years since that summit.

God answered my questions. "Yes, it was worth all the expense, time, and energy. Yes, the friendships continue to grow. Yes, unity is growing. Yes, His Kingdom continues to be built and strengthened. Yes, yes, yes!"

This story deals only with nine women and tells where God has taken them. I think of the thousands of other women whose lives were touched by God at the Women's Prayer Summits, but whose stories have not been heard, and I wonder, *Where has God taken them? What has He done in their lives? What is He doing in their lives?*

Maybe, after reading the following chapters from the Executive Committee, they will tell us their stories. I have no doubt but that they are equally thrilling as the chapters that lie ahead. This is the secret!

WHAT CAN ONE WOMAN DO?
She can do anything God wants to do through her.

CHAPTER THREE

The Harvest Spreads to Queens, Africa, and Jamaica

(BEVERLY CAESAR)

ARE NOT ALL ANGELS

MINISTERING SPIRITS

SENT TO SERVE THOSE WHO WILL

INHERIT SALVATION?

—HEBREWS 1:14

The doctor cocked his head as he watched the young man and woman. The gait of their steps alerted him. As they approached the gate leading to his office in the little house in Jamaica, West Indies, they hesitated, stopped as if reconsidering, and then turned to open the gate. Something about the pretty young woman caught his attention. He closed his eyes, wondering if he was imagining what he thought he'd seen. Opening his eyes and looking again, yes, it was a light . . . as a halo, it encircled her.

His furrowed brow and drawn mouth betrayed his bewilderment as he opened the door. Uncharacteristically, he walked rapidly toward the couple. His words shocked them: "Stop. Go home and have this baby."

The young couple turned around and returned to the two little children at their tiny dwelling. They had not wanted to come for an abortion. Neither one had been comfortable with this choice, but it had seemed the only way out. They were behind in their rent, their utilities had been turned off, and food was always in short supply. When they had discovered another baby was on the way, they panicked. Now, however, they would have to find a way.

And they did. Or, to be more accurate . . . God found a way!

A beautiful baby girl was born, and they named her Beverly. God began to reveal himself to the baby's mother, Veronica. She placed her trust in Jesus as her Savior and Lord, and her newfound faith began to flourish. It gave her the courage to move to the United States with her children. Her husband, still a stranger to the faith, followed.

This is the history surrounding the natural birth of the amazing woman Beverly Caesar. She is alive today because the hand of a personal God intervened in the circumstances of her life when she was a fetus of two months in her mother's womb.

God gave me the privilege to meet this woman of faith at our first focus group in Flushing Meadows, New York. The tall, slender, attractive woman and her husband made a striking statement as they entered. They displayed no airs, but it was evident they both lived "life with purpose."

In conversation after our focus group, I discovered several revealing facts about Beverly. It was evident that she had "caught the vision" of a prayer assembly. It was also obvious that she was a woman who prayed and that her prayers had been answered in miraculous ways. Her dedication to the development and education of her children through home schooling was apparent. As I observed her that day, I quickly decided she was a woman I wanted to know better.

God graciously granted my request. On December 12, 1996, she officially joined the Executive Committee to become the fourth member of our team, where she served as Minister of Outreach for both prayer summits. She was a perfect fit for motivating women, pastors, and all the churches to "Come to the Garden."

Beverly never failed to be an encouragement. Her inspiration certainly did not end with the Women's Prayer Summits. The places and ministries to which God has led her in the past decade have continued to thrill and inspire me. Whatever He has asked of her, she steps up, "ready for duty."

I interviewed Beverly twice for this book. The first interview occurred six years after the first prayer summit, and the second interview was four years later—ten years after the first prayer summit. I have asked that she tell you, in her own words, how God spoke to her through the prayer summit process and to share the effects of that influence upon her life, ministry, and church.

SIX YEARS AFTER THE FIRST PRAYER SUMMIT

"The fact that sparked my interest at our first meeting, before the committee was formed, was that a woman who was not known to New York, somebody whose name was not a household name, wanted to step out on faith into such a big project in New York City in bringing women together. That impressed me, because I saw a woman who was either crazy or who had heard from God. After meeting you, I knew that God had spoken to you. So, I said to myself, 'I've got to see this thing to the end, see this thing through, to see how it will end up!'

"I considered myself a novice when I came onto the committee. I came in as Roderick's wife, a new pastor, so I was feeling my way. 'Pastoring' was new to me. Prior to that I was active in the women's ministry as the president of the Women's Auxiliary, but my ministry was limited to my church.

"The awe we experienced as some of the abilities—that we didn't know we possessed—were pulled out of us as we served on the committee left us praising God. We were seven women from different denominational experiences and backgrounds. The harmony the seven of us had was wonderful. We were coming together to pull thousands of women from all walks of life under one roof to worship the Lord. I was open for the Lord to do what He wanted to do. Now what did He do? He blew us out of the water! He gave us above and beyond what we expected. It was a won-der-ful experience! Absolutely wonderful!

"Our petitions to God asked that our words would strike home, so that when the women left The Theater At Madison Square Garden, they wouldn't leave the same as they came. They would say, 'I came to the Garden, and I met Jesus.' Yes, we knew that the Holy Spirit would do the job, and from testimony that I received, I know that is what happened.

"Some of the women from Westbury, our branch church, had powerful testimonies, *life-changing* testimonies. One woman in particular brought her daughter. During the summit, as they were sitting together, they looked out over the crowd at the diversity from all the different denominations: white women, Asian women, African women, Hispanic women, and West Indian women. They were holding hands and singing together and worshiping God. My friend thought, *These people can hold hands, and they don't know one another; and here I am at odds with my daughter, who came from me. I must change that! Why can't I love my daughter and forgive her?* It turned her life around! Yes, there were many women, but that one rings out to me because it happened at the very first prayer summit as we focused on reconciliation. That was powerful!

"Another amazing thing is that women still ask, 'When are we going to have another prayer summit?' For example, my husband and I were vacationing in California five years after the first summit and speaking to each other in an elevator. A woman was standing in front of us facing the elevator door. When she heard my husband's voice, she turned around and asked if he was Bishop Caesar, the pastor she heard daily on the radio. Upon his affirmative answer, she asked if I was his wife. When he answered yes, she looked straight to me and with a voice filled with emotion said, 'Well, when are you going to do another prayer summit? Oh, that was awesome.' "

Beverly stated her conviction that the power in the Women's Prayer Summit was because the women didn't come to the Garden to see a person, another human. They were invited to come to see deity—to meet Jesus. She continued, "That's why the marquee read: *Come meet Jesus*. Women came, and they saw seven regular women, just like themselves. They saw the genuineness of our hearts and that we meant to speak to Jesus and to see Him, and to see Him alone. That is what impacted them. They didn't see plush . . . fashion . . . a lot that made them think, *Oh, I cannot attain that.*

"And they heard testimonies from women to whom they could relate and who spoke clearly to their hearts. They saw something that was attainable, something they could embrace and take home. We offered them Jesus. That's why they were impacted; that's why they want another prayer summit.

"At the Women's Prayer Summit, we prayed, and people saw that it really was a prayer meeting. In our local church, our prayer breakfasts would always end with a guest speaker or preacher coming and preaching, and there really wasn't much prayer. Because of what we saw at the Women's Prayer Summit, our people have requested that when we have a prayer breakfast, that we pray. Now, we have prayer breakfasts four times a year, and we pray! The format we use is similar to what we used in the Theater. We lift the issues we want to pray for before the Lord—the government, challenges of the church, or whatever. In our church, those two things are a direct result of the prayer summit."

THE PERSONAL IMPACT OF THE PRAYER SUMMIT

"The effect of the Women's Prayer Summit upon my personal walk has played a key role in my life today, years later. Life has taken on new meaning. I remember a couple of times when we were talking on the telephone, and we would just stop and pray. I have adopted that posture. Praying the Scriptures is in my spirit. When I am talking to a young woman on the phone, or if I am in counsel with a wife and she reaches a point where I think we need prayer, I no longer hesitate—we stop and pray.

"And, on a corporate level, my inhibitions have been taken away. Where I was once fearful and thought I could not embark upon a project that seemed too overwhelming and too massive, I now have a mind-set of faith. What seven women could do has propelled me to think outside the box. I have learned to take God out of the box.

"After the summit, many doors opened for me—wide open! Ministry mushroomed. I don't recall doing anything outstanding at the prayer summit, but I was given new opportunities to minister in a wide spectrum of churches. I was invited into Presbyterian, Baptist, Lutheran, even charismatic Catholic churches, and Pentecostal churches.

"Since I crossed over into my fifties, I have experienced an urgency in my spirit and in my belly. I have written my memoirs,

Experiencing the 25th Hour. I wrote *Looking for Love*, a musical based on the narrative of the woman at the well (John 4), and put it into a contemporary setting. We adapted it for Halloween and presented it on Halloween at York College Performing Arts Center that seats fifteen hundred people. It sold out, and the wonderful report is that more than fifty people came to the altar for salvation! More than fifty people walked down that long aisle to say, "I need Jesus, who can change my life." God birthed this fabulous play in me. We have been invited to take the play to Long Island, Brooklyn, to all the boroughs, and Florida.

"God is still working with this musical! I so wanted the music and songs to be original music, but we had to get permission to use three songs for our first presentation.

"People in our church had written three songs for us, but I was still hopeful. After the first performance of the musical, we were on vacation, and one morning I prayed, 'Lord, You know I don't write music or lyrics,' and He asked, 'Why not?' I asked if He would give me the lyrics, and He did! He gave me words to the additional three songs I needed: "Looking for Love," a second song dealing with "Time," and a third song, "Forgiven." In all, God gave me six original songs—ORIGINAL. God gave me the lyrics for three songs, but I still didn't have the music."

The morning of this interview an amazing thing had happened to Beverly on the way to meet with me. I was so excited that I could be part of what God was continuing to impart into her life. I, a noncharismatic believer, had seen Him speak to her many times during the two years we worked together on the Women's Prayer Summit. Therefore, her experience of that morning, while thrilling, didn't surprise me as it once might have. As we talked, she was exploding with joy and amazement. And as soon as I heard what happened, so was I!

Driving her car, while fighting the New York City morning traffic, she had been talking with God. She had said, "God, NO, I am not a musician. NO, I don't write music. NO, I don't play an instrument. I don't . . . " She paused for a moment, then she looked at me and continued, "BUT, He gave me the beat, the rhythm for the songs. I was crying while driving down the street, and I can't wait to get home to my musical daughters. I am going to sit down with them to give them what I am feeling. I am hearing the violin, the trumpet—I am hearing all the instruments. I have never experienced this before. Talk about birthing and not limiting God or putting Him in a box—this is it!"

But there was much more going on in her life. She was directing a full cantata with drama at their church, involving all the Sunday school departments, the Worship, Art, and Drama departments, and a big cast of men and women—shepherds, angels, kings, and all. She went on, "I tell you, I am not limiting God."

No, a woman whose birth was dependent upon God's personal intervention knows firsthand the truth of 2 Chronicles 16:9a: *For the eyes of the Lord search back and forth across the whole earth, looking for people whose hearts are perfect toward Him, so that He can show His great power by helping them* (Living Bible).

Her book, *Experiencing the 25th Hour,* is about prayer and a miracle-working God. The story of their son's birth and his survival against all odds will thrill everyone who reads it.

Their church, Bethel Gospel Tabernacle, Queens, New York, is a praying church. For fifty years the church has been opened every morning at six o'clock for one hour of prayer, and every Thursday has been designated a day of prayer. When Beverly's husband, Bishop Roderick Caesar, became pastor, he added fasting. Twice a year the whole church has three days of consecration and fasting as a corporate body.

Beverly shared that the value of the Women's Prayer Summit, even for a praying church such as theirs, reinforced for their women the importance and power of *united* prayer. Though they had already been praying and fasting, the model that the Women's Prayer Summit established could be used to encourage other ministries and other churches in these essentials.

When Beverly was asked to write her play, she fasted and prayed, asking God for direction. She and her husband were on vacation when the Lord gave her the idea for the play, and He gave the lyrics for the songs when they were on vacation at a later date. Because the production was scheduled for Halloween, such a crucial time, she called the whole cast in for prayer, to bombard heaven for all the members in the cast. They prayed that people would follow Jesus. Before the performance, the whole cast fasted for one full day, and they saw the results when the seekers came walking down the aisle.

Beverly said, "I believe that if we fast, pray, and consecrate a project that God has given to us, God is going to open the doors and make it successful.

"I thought the prayer summit was a B-I-G undertaking that was almost impossible, but I met a woman who said, 'No, no.'

I said, 'If God can do that, and we have such a successful prayer summit, *I am not going to put Him in a box anymore. I am taking the cover off. His power is limitless.*' "

TEN YEARS AFTER THE FIRST PRAYER SUMMIT

In 2007, four years after the above statement, ten years after the first prayer summit, I caught up with Beverly. She was preparing to leave for the National Religious Broadcasters (NRB) annual meeting with her husband, a member of the board. Let's take a look at what God has done since she took the cover off His box to allow His power to overflow.

As I began to interview Beverly, she reiterated the influence of the Women's Prayer Summit upon her everyday life of prayer, as she had stressed four years earlier. "I realize there is no matter too mundane or unimportant to forego prayer over it. The seemingly most insignificant situation can quickly turn into something very serious. I seize every moment and every situation to pray!"

"What about your book, *Experiencing the 25th Hour?*" I asked.

"Oh, I am receiving many letters and feedback. God is using it in the lives of women. The words I hear most often are *reconciliation* and *healing*. The deliverance the women are writing about covers every imaginable situation. I praise God for using it in this way."

She is writing her second book on marriage relationships.

God downloaded her first play into her mind in answer to her request, and He has given her a second, *The Journey,* and yet a third. The response to *The Journey* equaled that of her first play. *David and Bathsheba—Lust, Lies, and Mercy,* scheduled for three productions in October 2007, is her third play.

The March of Dimes held their first faith-based summit covering preterm births in Queens, New York, in 2005. Beverly was asked to be the keynote speaker. She is now an official volunteer to bring awareness to the African-American community to deal with preterm births and was delegated as a Family Team Captain for the April 2007 "March of Dimes Walk America" around Flushing Meadows Park, New York.

In the midst of all these outreach events, the thrust of her Lord prompted her return to the country of her birth. A young believer, Carone Gordon, a prayer warrior for the country of Jamaica, caught the hearts of Beverly and her husband. They go back each year to hold revival services. In addition, their church provides almost the complete support for a clinic and a nursing home in Jamaica in conjunction with a local church.

The thrust propelled onward to Uganda, Rwanda, and Kenya, on the continent of Africa, where Beverly's heart was broken. They went into such remote villages that they had to walk when their four-wheel drive vehicles could go no farther. But they were determined to minister to women in those countries who have no future on earth, but who have the assurance of an eternity with Christ in heaven. They are HIV/AIDS women.

They visited villages where the majority of the households were headed by children and learned that $30 would support a child for a month. Beverly came home, promoted, and arranged a fund-raiser, "Hope Concert," for the sponsor, World Vision, at York College Performing Arts Center. Choirs from Queens, Brooklyn, and Manhattan sang. Over six hundred women attended; most of them were from Bethel. They raised a good amount of support for World Vision to send back to Africa, and one hundred and fifty women each signed up to sponsor a child.

The overflowing source of power as seen in Beverly's life has led her back to rejoin the faculty of Bethel Bible Institute (BBI), where she teaches "The Ministry of Prayer." BBI was founded sixty years ago by the late Bishop Roderick Caesar and was the first Bible institute on Long Island. Today, it is an accredited college through ACI and offers Bachelor of Theology degrees through Vision International. Extension facilities are in Amityville and Roosevelt, Long Island: Monticello, New York; Port of Spain, Trinidad; Kerela, India; Barbados; Johannesburg, South Africa; and Managua, Nicaragua.

Beverly's priorities are her fellowship with her Lord and her devotion to her husband, children, grandchild, and extended family. Her ministries flow from a woman who has learned that the way up and out come from a bended knee to Almighty God, our Lord Jesus Christ. We repeat her affirmation: "I have learned to take God out of the box."

WHAT CAN BEVERLY CAESAR DO?
Anything God wants to do through her!

WHAT CAN YOU DO?
Anything God wants to do through you!

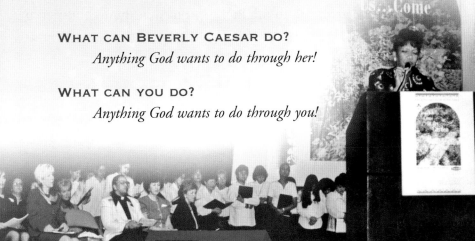

CHAPTER FOUR

Other Cities—
Other Nations

(BEVERLY COOK)

"THE SALARY WAS A LITTLE MORE

THAN FIFTY PERCENT CUT IN

PAY FROM MY LAST JOB.

WAS I INTERESTED IN SUCH A

POSITION? YOU BET!"

What could motivate a single "professional woman" to make such a statement? Particularly a woman who had taken great pride in her career?

This is how Beverly Cook explains it: "As a professional woman, I had achieved much of what my parents, the civil rights activists of the '60s, and the feminists of the '70s had fought for—a college education, a career, a wonderful apartment, good friends, and financial independence. I had even had a few love relationships by which to judge my ideal mate. Yet by the age of twenty-nine, I realized that all this was vanity, all this was meaningless (Ecclesiastes 1:2).

"The epitome of the American dream belonged to me, but I began to realize this was an empty existence. This professional woman needed to know the meaning of life. What was my purpose? What would bring fulfillment? Especially since I realized the latest boyfriend was *not* to be my husband. If my goal to be married by thirty was to be achieved, there must be something greater to take its place.

"I searched for several months, following clues of what others had found meaningful. A friend trusted in the power of crystals, so I tried them but soon found this wasn't enough to fulfill me. I knew many African-Americans were following the Muslim faith, so I read Malcolm X's autobiography in an attempt to understand that religion. I was impressed by the discipline of its devotees, yet I did not feel this faith expression was for me. Astrology and numerology also did not provide the lifestyle impact for which I was searching. Alone in my kitchen on a Sunday afternoon, my heart cried out to God to truly know the meaning of life.

"Unbeknownst to me, my roommate and a coworker of mine were praying I might find the answers—in Jesus. And, boy, did I! On New Year's Day, January 1, 1992, I accepted Christ into my heart as my personal Savior. I finally understood that a man named Jesus had actually lived on earth as both man and God, unconfused, in one body. He had died for my sins, risen from the dead, ascended into heaven, and sits at the right hand of God, having sent the Holy Spirit to dwell with us in this present age! This all made perfect sense to me—a faithful devotee of science fiction.

"However, what was my first question as to how I was to live out my faith? 'Can I still watch *Star Trek*?' Whoa, do you see where my priorities were? 'Yes, that is fine,' I was told, 'and you can still wear makeup and pants!' Praise God for His grace and wisdom offered to me by my two sisters in Christ, and for immediately planting me in a God-fearing church, where I began to grow in my faith."

TAKING THE BIG STEP OF FAITH

"Upon being *born again,* the Holy Spirit instilled within me a desire to only be about 'my Father's business,' as the young Jesus is quoted as saying in Luke 2 (KJV). The Lord had given me a vision of working for Him in, through, and for churches. I wanted to combine the gifts and talents He had given me with the knowledge and experience I had learned in the secular world of corporate public relations in New York City.

"During a time of transition in 1995, the Lord placed me in the nerve center of the Christian universe in the city, working on the city-wide *March for Jesus* (the most spectacular evangelistic parade you've ever seen) out of the New York Bible Society office in Manhattan. Occasionally, I would see the most beautiful classy women ascend the staircase of our brownstone for meetings I knew not of. I only knew I wanted to join them, to be in the company of what appeared to be such godly dynamic women. Little did I know I would have the privilege of joining them in just over a year.

"I volunteered to manage the administrative needs of the *March for Jesus* that year and met several of the city's spiritual gatekeepers. There really is nothing like the feeling one gets seeing all the pieces come together for a major event—the untold hours served by men and women committed to the cause of Christ to reach every man, woman, and child with the Gospel. It was a glorious morning!

"The day of the march, I met the Rev. Mac Pier, leader of the prayer rally that culminated the event, and God's plan for my life was put into motion. (It really had been in motion all along. I just wasn't aware of it.) Later Rev. Pier asked me to work on another special event, coming up that September, for the Body of Christ in New York City. I was unaware that these were the days the Lord began birthing a new thing through His servant Janet Broling, who was living across the river in New Jersey.

"Early in 1996, Pastor Mac approached me about this woman, Janet, and God's vision for a day of prayer and praise for all believing women at one of the most famous theaters in the region. As the director of what was then the Urban Strategy Division of Concerts of Prayer International, Mac Pier and this ministry were uniquely positioned by God to mobilize pastoral support for such an ambitious endeavor. However, a full-time staff worker was going to be required to administrate this event.

" 'Would you be interested in such a position?' Pastor Mac asked me. The salary was a little more than a fifty percent cut in pay from my last job. But it was a chance to work for God; to mobilize women across race, age, denomination, and economic barriers—for the glory of God. Would I be interested? You bet I was interested!"

THE MOST DIFFICULT PUBLIC RELATIONS ASSIGNMENT EVER

There was a possibility Beverly would be working for both the Women's Prayer Summit and Concerts of Prayer for Greater New York, so we met for lunch at a quaint little restaurant overlooking the skating rink at Rockefeller Square to become acquainted. I was intrigued with this young woman. She exuded poise and a quiet dignity. And every so often a tear would overflow her big brown eyes and roll down onto her cheek, revealing a softness and latent emotions not readily apparent from casual observances and verbal interactions. By the time we had finished our lunch, I felt I knew Beverly Cook well enough to know that she would be a great asset to help bring about the Women's Prayer Summit. She began working on the Women's Prayer Summit in March 1996.

"As it turned out, I split my work week between the Women's Prayer Summit and Concerts of Prayer. Our first order of business was to mobilize the Executive Committee. And who should comprise that committee? Dynamic women whom I recognized from those meetings at the Bible Society and from local Christian media—Dixie Galloway, Beverly Caesar, etc.!

"When I began work in vocational ministry, it was because I felt called by God to bring the gifts and talents He'd bestowed upon me for His use in the Body of Christ (1 Corinthians 10:31). I realized I was not perfect, nor that I knew everything. Yet I was *proud* (get it?) of the knowledge I possessed. What struck me about vocational ministry was how so many offices seemed to be run contrary to traditional business practices. Everything was left to God to think through rather than being planned to the smallest detail. Long-range planning generally was not implemented.

"Would the Women's Prayer Summit be run in similar fashion? I wondered—*completely on faith?* I was pleased to find that faith and careful management would share equal importance in producing this event. In fact, even the smallest detail was considered so important to the plan, because it could mean the difference between remaining in budget or having to pay a penalty of thousands of dollars. But there also was a deep certainty of our reliance on the Lord and His being at work in all we did.

"The unique challenge about this event was that there would be no tangible headliner, no superstar speaker. Even at our business meetings, the head chair at the conference table was left vacant—symbolic that Christ was the head of our committee. The clarion call was being sounded by our Lord Jesus Christ alone. The Holy Spirit was the publicist and recruiter of those who attended. This was so contrary to what I had been taught in the 'professional' world! This was the most difficult public relations assignment I had ever encountered. This challenged my 'professional' sensibilities! Yet, I endeavored to live and learn what I could through this process."

And "live and learn" is exactly what Beverly did. She played a double role for the Women's Prayer Summit. She was the only person who received remuneration because of her status as a "faith missionary" with Concerts of Prayer. And she was the only Executive Committee Member involved in each of the focus groups. She and Joni organized them. In addition, she participated in each of our mini-prayer summits and in every ministry leaders' meeting. On the day of the Women's Prayer Summit, she played a vital role in the "Reconciliation" aspect of the program. In addition, she served as a board member of our corporation, the Women's Prayer Summit, Inc.

When God so blessed the first prayer summit and made it clear that there was to be a second Women's Prayer Summit, Concerts of Prayer volunteered Beverly's time on the committee. We moved our office to Harlem and were able to employ Diana Doleman as full-time administrator—at the same high salary! Bethel Gospel Assembly provided office and conference room spaces to us—free. That enabled Beverly to devote all her time to our public relations needs. What a wonderful gift!

THE HARVEST SPREADS TO OTHER CITIES

After the last Women's Prayer Summit in October 1998, Beverly continued to serve the Lord with Concerts of Prayer—Greater New York as communications director.

In the past ten years, God has continued to stretch and develop her skills through many national events that have brought

Christian leaders from around the country to New York City. The purpose is for them to gain exposure to some of the things that are happening in the metropolitan New York City area and to learn how the Gospel can be taken in different ways to different sectors of urban society. New York leaders are also able to hear what is happening around the country. This cross-pollination results in the leaders taking the best practices and contextualizing them to meet the needs in their ministries and cities.

Beverly said, "Believers have to be a source of light and salt in each sector of society. We cannot avoid any segment of the populace. We must take the initiative and bring the Gospel to various areas, such as the business community, political arena, or education. We can't leave society to its own resources, but we have to come and share the Gospel's perspective. We must be able to influence society toward those things that will benefit people of all backgrounds and always be alive with the principles that we, as believers, understand. We do not impose our morality on others, but hopefully they will see and understand that Christ's ways of life are more beneficial than the ways they are living. Then, it is our prayer their hearts and minds will be opened to the Gospel of Jesus.

"The Christian Community Development Association national conference was hosted in New York City in 2000. Workshops to help influence various parts of society were located throughout the city and covered such topics as youth ministry, prison ministry, men's ministry, and various aspects of the church. At every point we tried to ensure there was racial and denominational diversity among the speakers and throughout the worship. We were at a Korean church with a primarily Korean-speaking congregation. It was a wonderful taste of heaven. Although the body of believers could not understand the words their wonderful choir was singing, we understood the Lord's part and His love being expressed through the many voices of the choir.

"We always try to take the people outside of the meeting venue to see what is actually happening around the city and in the various ministries. At the National Leadership Forum in October 2004, we had twenty-two different learning tracts, and we met in appropriate venues of society that we were trying to address. For example, the Media and Entertainment Tract met at the Salvation Army location right there in the theater district. We also had speakers who came and shared their faith through their work in the entertainment arena. They told of how believers are making a difference and are reaching out to cultural and business leaders in the entertainment field.

"The Compassion Tract met for two days at Bowery Mission in Manhattan and at Love Gospel Assembly in the Bronx, so that people could see compassion in action. Each of these locations has a wonderful feeding ministry. You can't see that in a room. You can see it on video, but there is nothing like being there.

"Bethel Gospel Assembly in Harlem hosted the Missions Tract. Bethel is a black church that reaches out to the uttermost parts of the world and in the United States to get the Gospel out to people of all races—to people who don't look like them and who are of different cultures."

Prior to these events, you will find Beverly producing promotional materials, videos, journals, and in mobilizing some of the leaders to come. On the day of the event or during it, she is usually working behind the scenes with the special guests, speakers, and all public relations.

THE HARVEST SPREADS TO OTHER NATIONS

"In May 2002, I was part of a vision trip to Uganda and Rwanda. I spent a week in each country, observing the work of World Vision. We began to partner with this ministry in October 2001, right after the events of 9/11. Our relationship with them at that time was to assist those who had been affected by the World Trade Center tragedy in New York City. Following that, we began to get involved in their work in combating the AIDS/HIV virus in Africa. Each day six thousand children are being orphaned. We understand that if the pandemic continues at the pace it is now, by the year 2010 there could be from twenty-five to forty million orphans in Africa.

"Uganda has experienced a huge drop in the number of newly HIV affected people. The reasons given for that are prayer and the churches working with government in what they call the ABC's—abstinence, behavioral change, and condoms. So they recognize that if they are not going to be abstinent or change their behavior, the last resort is condoms.

"We also went to Rwanda, which had experienced one hundred days of major genocide from April 6 to mid July 1994. Estimates range from five hundred thousand to between eight hundred thousand and a million deaths. They are in the process of rebuilding their country. While we were there, they voted upon their constitution at only the second democratic election since the genocide had ended. Rwandans waved their inked thumbs as we drove past one polling site. As a beneficiary of America's civil rights movement, I felt privileged to experience such a powerful move of democracy. This was a sign of hope after such inhumane devastation.

"After returning home, we had a women's luncheon to try to mobilize women leaders around the issue of supporting widows and orphans in Africa. We had a one hundred-day campaign to try to raise one thousand child sponsorships—modeled after the one hundred days that the genocide had happened. We want to help turn that country around. That is another way I have been involved in what God is doing in the church."

BEVERLY COOK IN 2007

That was Beverly's heart as expressed in December 2003. Has it changed in 2007? No, it still responds to the same drummer—*Jesus*.

While Beverly spends the majority of her days in New York City and in the greatly expanded ministry of Concerts of Prayer, she is actively planning as to how she might prepare herself to be of help, someday, in Uganda as an elementary teacher. The plight of the young people in that country tugs at her mind and emotions. She returned to Uganda in 2004 and hopes to mobilize a team from her church to go back for another trip.

As the future of any country lies in its youth, the same is true of any family. Beverly has carried a great concern for her nephews since I have known her. This past Christmas, when she had returned to her home city of Atlanta, she discovered that her two young nephews are Christians. She gave them the kids' version of *My Utmost for His Highest* by the late Oswald Chambers. They agreed that she will phone them once a month so that in this way she may disciple them. She holds high expectations for the spiritual vitality of her family, including her parents.

Remember that "March" that really pulled Beverly into ministry? Well, she is still actively involved in a management role. The event has become the "Pray New York! Prayer-Walk." Rather than one centralized event, believers are dispersed throughout the city. The first Saturday of June 2006, seven thousand people from over three hundred churches adopted one of the more than two hundred zip codes of the metropolitan New York City area to prayer-walk. They prayed for blessings from Christ upon the leaders, youth, and marriages. They prayed for God's manifest presence upon everyone in that city. In 2007, the fourth year of the prayer-walk, their goal is for eight thousand people to prayer-walk the city, and they are extending the walk from the first Saturday to every Saturday in June. As a practical application of Luke 10, healing services will be held at participating churches. The church in the metropolitan New York City area continues to pray and work together.

The Billy Graham Crusade held in Flushing Meadows in June 2005 was a prime example of the blessings God pours upon His people when they gather to pray and worship as one voice in the Name of Jesus. Beverly and Dr. Pier invited me and my husband to come and experience what may have been the last crusade of Dr. Graham. I volunteered to pray during one of the meetings, and my designated area was the farthest from the big screen and stage where Dr. Graham preached on Youth Night. There I witnessed something that you may find difficult to imagine.

One hundred and fifty thousand people were estimated to be in attendance Saturday night. The youth were everywhere, and so were the police. But the police had nothing to do. Can you imagine that many people, mostly young people, sitting in huge open outside areas, and no one is causing any disturbance? They listened to the music, to peers who gave witness of what Jesus Christ had done in their lives, and to the Word of God as spoken by Dr. Graham. As I sat there, I thought to myself, *I would never have believed this could happen had I not seen it with my own eyes.* I also wondered, *Will the press write about this phenomenon?*

Beverly will also be working behind the scenes during a national conference planned for September 2007 in New York City commemorating the one hundred-and-fifty-year anniversary of the Fulton Street Noon Prayer Meetings formerly led by Jeremiah Lamphier. These prayer meetings precipitated the great revival in New York City that began in the marketplace and spread coast to coast. The participants prayed for salvation for specific individuals in their spheres of influence and for the Holy Spirit's empowerment. The prayer goal is for a repeat of those days with one thousand pastors and leaders participating.

Beverly's involvement with two other new entities to spread the good news of Jesus Christ ranges from various behind-the-scenes roles: prayer teams, promotion, media involvement, and organization. Concerts of Prayer is birthing a leadership center to train leaders from New York City and from around the country about urban and global missions. The goal is to encourage united prayer, church planting, global compassion, and leadership development in other American cities. Vision New York is a network connected with eighteen denominations to establish churches in the city.

BECOMING A FULFILLED SINGLE WOMAN

As we wrapped up our interview, I asked Beverly, "You are still single. Is there any specific individual?" She let me know the practicalities of some of the struggles of a single person.

"First, I am flabbergasted by God's audacity in my life to consider me worthy to be included in this book. What have I to say to bless other women? What would they find in my personal story that would touch their hearts and encourage them to greater things? Believe me, this is not false or true humility. This is the voice of insecurity, low self-esteem, and doubt that has been encouraged by one of Screwtape's demons (a character in C. S. Lewis's book *The Screwtape Letters*) whispering in my ear for most of my life. But because I have grown and matured much since those days, the demon is just an imp, an occasional nagging annoyance when I forget that 'the one who is in you is greater than the one who is in the world' (1 John 4:4).

"When I was a new believer, I was told, *Seek ye first the Kingdom of God and His righteousness and all these things will be added unto you.* I understood it intellectually and believed it, but I didn't know how to do it. Now I understand that you do it literally as it states. Seek God and His righteousness first—above all things, above everything, above your desire for a mate, above your career, and above your ministry! Do that first, and everything else will be added unto you. It has taken me a long time to learn that lesson. But ever since I have tried to do that, everything else has come.

"Regarding singleness, I have to know that my being single is for God's purpose. So if that is the case, what are the plans He wants me to do and fulfill? I will be listening. Because I met a faithful believer on my secular job long ago, today I am able to *Seek first the Kingdom of God*. So I try to encourage other believers to *live their faith* on the job.

"On a personal level, though, after the spiritual exhilaration of a big event, the married participants get to go home and share it with their mate. For the most part, my family and friends only share in my ministry from a distance. It is hard. For instance, on Valentine's Day there was no special man to share the day with, but I did get a beautiful bag."

"Tell me about it," I said.

"We were meeting to plan a fund-raiser for a ministry of my home church. The wife of the director had this cute bag, which I complimented her on. She said, 'Here it is, it's yours!' She got a plastic bag and dumped the contents of the bag in it and handed this lovely velvet bag to me. She then told me how someone had, at one time, done the same thing for her. Now," said Beverly, "I have to do the same thing for someone else. What I am really saying is that *The Lord is my valentine.*"

"The story of Isaac and Rebekah in Genesis 24 keeps me going. Though they were both single, neither of them was anxious about it. They were busy fulfilling God's present plan for their lives. They also spent time developing their personal relationship with God. So much so that they were able to recognize when He was calling them to fulfill a new role in their lives as a wife and a husband. Their story and Philippians 4:4–9 keep me hopeful yet satisfied with life as it is for now."

Beverly is moving confidently in faith. She and three friends have an accountability group, the M&M'S. They concentrate in prayer and actions upon their maison (French for *house*), money, movement (weight loss), and marital status (preparing to be good mates).

We ended our interview with a prayer of thanksgiving for Christ's personal manifestation of himself through His Holy Spirit in Beverly's life. Having known the joy of a wonderful husband in my life for almost fifty years, I also asked God to bring a special person into Beverly's life, one who will *love his wife as he loves himself* and whom *she may love and honor* (Ephesians 5:33). One with whom they both may more effectively serve the cause of our Lord Jesus Christ.

SINGLE OR MARRIED—WHAT CAN BEVERLY DO?
Anything God wants to do through her!

SINGLE OR MARRIED—WHAT CAN YOU DO?
Anything God wants to do through you!

CHAPTER FIVE

Reconciled to Bring Reconciliation

(DIXIE GALLOWAY)

SHE SAW IT HAPPEN OVERNIGHT!

BEFORE HER VERY EYES,

THE TRANSFORMING POWER OF

CHRIST JESUS WAS PORTRAYED.

IT WAS RADICAL!

When her cocaine-addicted, heavy alcohol-drinking husband repented, God supernaturally changed him overnight! Their lives were drastically changed. So Dixie possessed great faith in a personal, life-changing God.

I met this amazing woman in New York City. In a city with a population of more than eight million people and composed of five boroughs—Manhattan, Bronx, Brooklyn, Queens, and Staten Island—instant rapport between strangers is rare. The discovery of having grown up in the same home state of Oklahoma was a good beginning. We, however, shared a much greater connection. It created an immediate bond—our faith rooted in Jesus and in His power!

There was something else going on when God allowed our paths to cross in 1996. He had placed a task within the mind and heart of each of us. Our respective tasks were interrelated. One task focused upon a goal; the other task spotlighted the One who could bring about that goal.

You have already read about my assignment—an assembly in, possibly, the most well-known venue in the world, The Theater At Madison Square Garden. The headliner—the focus—*Jesus!*

What was Dixie Galloway's focus? *Unity!* Unity in the Body of Christ. Racial unity. Denominational unity. Unity in the powerful Name of Jesus!

What kind of woman would God trust with that focus? Well, Dixie was a woman full of vitality!

Whenever she walked into a room, her short blonde hair, lively personality, purposeful bearing, and flair demonstrated her vigor. Driving a spotless 1948 Chevy hotrod, she was not easily forgotten! But there is much more to her story.

Dixie and her husband, Richard, met in college, but a tour in Vietnam interrupted their education. At the end of the tour, they returned to college, completed their education, and then began a business that grew to become very successful financially. However, personally and spiritually, it brought disaster. They lived near the Haight-Ashbury District of San Francisco, and as they became more affluent, drugs were added to their lives. Devastating drugs!

Dixie said, "Even though I wasn't totally given over to the drugs, Richard gradually became more and more controlled by cocaine and alcohol. Our kids' ages were ten, five, and one, and I became very concerned for their welfare.

"God used the occasion of my aunt's death to get my attention. *He reminded me that He is real, and that there is a heaven. What we see here is not the only thing that is going on.* I came back to Him— all the way back! I confessed my sins, and He forgave me. I had grown up in the Baptist church and knew who Jesus was, but I just had not thought about Him for quite a few years. I began to study my Bible again, and over a period of months I was able to confront Richard, 'All this is not pleasing to God. It has to change.'

"When Richard repented, God supernaturally changed him overnight! He had been doing a huge quantity of drugs and alcohol. It all made me sick, so I was not that heavily into it. But when Richard stopped drinking the alcohol and using cocaine, our lives drastically changed."

THE TRANSFORMATION CONTINUES

"We immediately thought, *Let's get away—take a trip.* So we went to the Virgin Islands. By the time we returned home, we had decided to sell everything and begin anew in the Virgin Islands, to just see where God would lead us.

"Within three months from Richard's life-changing meeting with God, we had sold our business, our home, and everything we owned that was saleable, and moved to the Virgin Islands to follow after God. We were so tightly focused upon God that He restored our fractured family. In less than a year, Richard's family came to visit, and they joined us in the prayer meetings and the Bible study we had begun.

"For two years we studied the Bible and worshiped God. In the midst of this we began to do some outreach—going into homes and into the streets to witness about the grace of God. Many people became believers in Christ. In the beginning, they met in our home, but eventually we became a church. When God led us from the Virgin Islands to Puerto Rico, the local believers took over the church leadership.

"In Puerto Rico, we were asked to establish a television station. It was really Richard's baby. Two years later it went on the air and is still operating today. Puerto Rico has a twenty-four-hour Christian station that reaches a population of over two million people.

"Ironically, while Richard was working on starting the television station, I felt that God wanted me to put together a program for women. Richard thought I was *crazy.* Here we were in Puerto Rico, birthing a television station, and I was going to travel back and forth to St. Thomas and have to pay for all the time?

"I said, 'Well, they probably won't want me anyway. They don't have any Christian television in that area. If they say no, I will be off the hook.' But they said yes.

"So I did an interview talk show for six months from St. Thomas. It was called, *Let Go and Let God.* I interviewed various believers and inquired, 'How did you come to know God?' and 'What has He done in your life?' "

Dixie revealed a surprising fact about her time on television. "It nearly killed me because I had terrible stage fright. That was the last thing *in the natural* that I felt gifted to do. When the show would come on the air, I watched it by myself because I was so embarrassed and humiliated by the standard of my performance. I was horrified by it. But I learned to speak publicly. Now I am comfortable. People can interview me, and I don't fall to pieces. It was just stepping out."

Puerto Rico was not their final destination. The next stop was the New York City area where they established New York City Relief, a food and benefit program for the homeless in the city and surrounding areas. New York City Relief buses distribute food and provide all kinds of help to the homeless and needy. In the process, they provide spiritual life through the Gospel.

When I met Dixie, she had been working five or six years with women to pursue her God-given task: "Unity in the body of Christ—racial unity—denominational unity—in the powerful Name of Jesus!" She hosted a monthly noon meeting for women ministry leaders in the metropolitan New York City area. They assembled to pray, fellowship, and give support to one another. Several times a year they planned special luncheons and seminars at various churches so that the many women of the ministries these women represented could come together. They represented different denominations, races, and ages.

TWO WOMEN AND TWO TASKS MEET

Word about a large women's gathering in one of the major secular venues in New York City reached Dixie early in 1996. Then for several months nothing happened. She said, "When I first heard about this, it seemed to fit perfectly with what I had been doing. I prayed to hear from God if this was something for me or New York City. Part of the call for Richard and me was to embrace and be a part of the whole Body, not just sit in one place. That is perfectly okay for other people, but that was just part of our calling."

God began to answer Dixie's prayer when she heard, firsthand, about the vision for the Women's Prayer Summit. She became the second woman to commit to join the Executive Committee of the Women's Prayer Summit, then she invited me to attend her monthly meetings for ministry leaders in New York City. We became good friends, but that friendship would be strained by conflict at times.

Dixie was experienced, and I considered myself a novice. Dixie knew many of the women ministry leaders and the pastors in the metropolitan New York City area, and I did not. She said,

"One of the biggest parts of my challenge was that my role was to submit to your leadership. I felt deeply that was a requirement from God; that's the way He does things." She was willing to submit to a woman unknown to the local church leaders and who was certain of only one thing—the focus of the Women's Prayer Summit was to be *Jesus*.

Dixie had a clearly defined goal that she felt the Women's Prayer Summit should pursue—*racial reconciliation*. She was not alone in this. The upcoming Promise Keepers Meeting for New York City was to be focused upon that goal. Some leaders in the city were also of this mind-set. Still others, including some of my sisters of color, felt differently. The big questions was: *How does Christ feel about this?*

I received a partial answer on October 12, 1996. It was a lovely luncheon at one of the magnificent churches on Fifth Avenue in New York City. The topic was prayer, and the morning had been filled with seminars, followed by lunch, special music, and then a panel to direct dialogue and answer questions. The mood of the morning was unusual. I have heard the comment, "I can always tell how well oiled a meeting is when I get up to speak. When the planning and the meeting have been saturated in prayer, there is freedom to speak and receptivity from those attending." This was one of those meetings.

After lunch, a soloist began to sing the words of Dick and Melodie Tunney: *We are sisters, sisters in the Lord; our faith in common, sisters in the Lord, no matter how the world defines us, nothing can break the tie that binds us; we are sisters in the Lord.* Her clear lovely voice was interrupted with the unmistakable sound of weeping. It came from one table, then from another, and another. It grew louder and louder as emotions gushed forth.

As soon as the solo was finished, Dixie quickly changed plans. She asked the panel members to come to the front of the room and invited the women to come forward for prayer. Many of the panel did not wait for the women to come forward but went over to the women's tables. A sister I approached sat completely rigid, in a catatonic state. We prayed, cried together, and shared long after the scheduled closing time.

CONFRONTING THE ELEPHANT IN THE ROOM

This was the beginning of a revelation to me of the deep pain with which many African-American and black women live. I would hear of being sent to the store to purchase something and of being ignored while others stepped in front of you. Yet, your parents had warned, "Don't say anything. It is dangerous!" One must deal with such treatment one way or another. Wounds buried deep within the heart and the emotions evoked are seldom, if ever, exposed. However, when they are, a force resembling a volcano erupts.

That day I realized the Women's Prayer Summit would have to deal with the issue of racial reconciliation. It was not just the African-American community that carried intense pain. It included the Hispanic, Asian, and Caucasian women as well. But I also knew that racial reconciliation could not be the focus of "Come to the Garden." *Jesus* was to be the focus. We would not focus on the problem. We would address the problem but focus on the One who could solve it, *Jesus!*

But how were we to handle this barrier that separated much of the Body of Christ? We had a tremendous advantage! The seven women of our Executive Committee were women in whom God had placed a longing to be part of the whole Body— not to dominate but to be directed by the Holy Spirit. It was God bringing those who had already been prepared and in whom He had awakened that deep desire.

God wanted to do something else. He wanted to break down ALL the barriers that existed in the Executive Committee, barriers of which we were unaware. But in time, He would reveal them to us. He had work to do among us before we could go to the women of the New York City metropolitan area.

There is no limit to what can bring division and separation in the Body of Christ: music, dress, personalities, traditions, education, money, on and on the list grows! However, we often overlook one of the reasons these small issues become big enough to divide us or cause conflict—*spiritual warfare!* Scripture tells us we have an opponent, a very powerful and ingenious adversary. But it also enlightens us as to how we may face and defeat this force—a reality in everyday life:

> PUT ON THE FULL ARMOR OF GOD SO THAT YOU CAN TAKE YOUR STAND AGAINST THE DEVIL'S SCHEMES. FOR OUR STRUGGLE IS NOT AGAINST FLESH AND BLOOD, BUT AGAINST THE RULERS, AGAINST THE AUTHORITIES, AGAINST THE POWERS OF THIS DARK WORLD AND AGAINST THE SPIRITU-AL FORCES OF EVIL IN THE HEAVENLY REALMS.

> THEREFORE PUT ON THE FULL ARMOR OF GOD, SO
> THAT WHEN THE DAY OF EVIL COMES, YOU MAY BE
> ABLE TO STAND YOUR GROUND, AND AFTER YOU
> HAVE DONE EVERYTHING, TO STAND.
>
> —EPHESIANS 6:11–13

We are given clear understanding of how the devil works and of what we are to do:

> BE SELF-CONTROLLED AND ALERT. YOUR ENEMY
> THE DEVIL PROWLS AROUND LIKE A ROARING LION
> LOOKING FOR SOMEONE TO DEVOUR. RESIST HIM,
> STANDING FIRM IN THE FAITH, BECAUSE YOU
> KNOW THAT YOUR BROTHERS THROUGHOUT THE
> WORLD ARE UNDERGOING THE SAME KIND OF
> SUFFERINGS.
>
> —1 PETER 5:8–9

The schemes of our enemy to derail all that God was going to do through the Women's Prayer Summit shifted into gear as the Executive Committee met to plan the summit program. We met for an evening and morning to fast and pray about the program. We had asked each woman to bring her suggested agenda. I shared my detailed plan and suggestions. By the time we parted on Saturday morning, I sensed there was no consensus, but nothing specific was verbalized. (It was our policy that if we did not have complete unity on any decision, we tabled it until God gave us a unanimous decision. If it didn't come, we didn't do it.)

At our regularly scheduled meeting the next week, we settled nothing.

Dixie was struggling with her assignment. She later told me, "As I was driving down the street in my old Chevy, I began to feel something well up within me. Tearful, I pulled over and stopped for a minute. I felt like I heard God say, *You are the one I called to stand on this point, and you are not to give way.* But I was not certain what I was not to give way to."

She had become frustrated because several times in our committee meetings she had raised the issue of how we would handle racial reconciliation, but no one responded. She said, "It was like an elephant in the living room that we don't talk about."

Actually, no one knew exactly how to handle this, so with no answer, we did nothing. God knew how He was going to handle it, though. He was working behind the scenes in response to those six mini-prayer summits, the forty days of rotational fasting and prayer, and the summer of prayer blitzes (see Chapter Two).

BREAKING DOWN BARRIERS IN THE BODY OF CHRIST

The following Monday, Dixie called me and said she would like to come over to talk before our regularly scheduled meeting in Harlem the next day. We had an afternoon of frank discussion that opened the door that God would use to restore our unencumbered fellowship.

Before she left, Dixie said, "I believe the reason I came into this had to do with the Body of Christ being in unity. You are the one in leadership. When it comes to unity, would you be willing to submit to me in that area if I have something?"

"Yes, but not on the day of the program."

"It is not about that."

Conflict sometimes arises over methodology, from misunderstandings due to a lack of communication for any number of reasons. There are times, however, when conflict arises because of sin. In our case, a misunderstanding had helped to create tension. Because I had not reacted as she expected, she thought I was opposed to addressing this issue. Clearly, I was not. I, on the other hand, was afraid Dixie wanted to shift the focus from *Jesus*. Clearly, she did not. But we had not communicated that to each other.

Dixie, at a later date, filled me in on the following: "After I got home from your house that day, I felt I got this unction from God. He gave me words to share the next day in our meeting, so I wrote them on a piece of paper. That was one of the most uncomfortable, unforgettable days of my life, but it was also very powerful. The next morning I called Wendie, our prayer director who gave a devotional at each meeting, and said, 'Wendie, God has something for me to share today, and it is in your place. Would you permit me?' And she agreed. I still had only the few words I had written down the day before. But when I went in the door, the Spirit of God came over me with enormous power. I had never experienced anything like it before."

In this meeting at Bethel Gospel Assembly in Harlem, as the Holy Spirit led our conversations and our prayers, the presence of God descended. He literally demolished other barriers within the members of the committee, barriers that we had no idea existed. Hearts opened, deep wounds were exposed, resentments shattered, tears flowed, and God gave forgiveness, understanding, and a love one for another that was phenomenal. Actually, it was a glimpse of what God was planning to do at the Women's Prayer Summit.

Years later, Dixie told me, "I felt the tears we all experienced that day were a confirmation to me that it has happened. This unity that I had been holding on for was like a spiritual entity, and I have never had anything come close to the experience I had that day. I called Richard after I left the meeting and said, 'I can't drive. I just had the most amazing experience with God, and I can't drive.' So he came and got me. It changed me forever."

Dixie's assignment and ours—reconciliation—comes from 2 Corinthians 5:17–19:

> THEREFORE, IF ANYONE IS IN CHRIST, HE IS A NEW CREATION; THE OLD HAS GONE, THE NEW HAS COME! ALL THIS IS FROM GOD, WHO RECONCILED US TO HIMSELF THROUGH CHRIST, AND GAVE US THE MINISTRY OF RECONCILIATION: THAT GOD WAS RECONCILING THE WORLD TO HIMSELF IN CHRIST, NOT COUNTING MEN'S SINS AGAINST THEM. AND HE HAS COMMITTED TO US THE MESSAGE OF RECONCILIATION.

Unexpectedly, at one of our next meetings, God gave His solution as to how we would handle the reconciliation feature of the program. When the idea came, everyone loved it, and one idea piled onto another. We all knew "this was the answer!" It was a simple skit with four women of different races, written by a member of Bethel Gospel Assembly. Dixie and Beverly Cook would follow with interviews of women of different cultures, letters of apology would be read, and then prayer time opened up so everyone in the Theater could participate.

Once unity was re-established in the committee, the barriers among us demolished, we were able to continue with the unrelenting details to bring about the Women's Prayer Summit. Ticket sales were under Joyce and Dixie. They had hordes of women all over the city working toward this goal.

As God had broken the barriers in our committee meeting, we were confident He would do the same thing during the Women's Prayer Summit in The Theater At Madison Square Garden. That is exactly what He did!

Dixie and I were faithful to our God-given tasks. The goal was achieved, but not without conflict. Conflict, however, is not necessarily a bad thing. It depends upon how it is handled. In fact, I firmly believe that whenever God wants to do a great work, it is safe to assume that conflict in some form will arise from our adversary. If we expect and prepare for it, we will be able to act rather than react. Conflict, left in the grip of our adversary, the devil, will divide and defeat the work our Lord desires. However, conflict saturated in prayer and accompanied by hearts, minds, and wills submitted to the commandments and supremacy of Jesus allows the Holy Spirit *to demolish the strongholds, arguments, and every pretension that sets itself up against the knowledge of God* (2 Corinthians 10:4).

As I interviewed Dixie for this chapter, she expressed it this way: "When it comes to power in prayer, and we are praying together, I refer to *the upper room* experience. At that time the full company of believers prayed *in one accord,* and God chose that moment to release Great Power on that day (Acts 4:23–31). I have felt that the power of God—released upon us, through us, and on New York City—was enhanced exponentially and immeasurably by the unity of the Spirit we enjoyed, first as a committee and as a diverse representation of the Body of Christ as we prayed together in The Theater At Madison Square Garden on October 4, 1997."

MINISTRY LIVES ON

Dixie shared how God has worked in her life since the Women's Prayer Summit. "Mostly, I have prayed—that has been part of my work. I credit the Women's Prayer Summit with my healing. During and after the Women's Prayer Summit, the doorways to all the secret places in me opened. That is one of the significant things that resulted in my life, which has involved an integration of my personality. If I am fearful on the inside, I no longer keep it hidden inside, but it is on the outside, too. If I am scared and something is really bothering me, I can say, 'I am really nervous about this. Pray for me.' Before, it was all boxed up somewhere, and that is no way to live."

As I was searching something on the Internet three years after I had moved from New York City, I read about The Call NYC and its director, Rodlyn Park. I immediately called her for more information. Rodlyn had faithfully served as the New Jersey ticket sales coordinator for the Women's Prayer Summit. She had sacrificially given up a part-time job in order to assume that role and did a tremendous job. Her prayer life, abilities, and dedication impressed everyone with whom she worked.

Dixie joined with Rodlyn and served as Prayer Chair and Liaison for The Call NYC, which covered two days of prayer and fasting in Flushing Meadows-Corona Park, Queens, NYC (adjacent to Shea Stadium and the U.S. Tennis Center). The first day of The Call NYC was Saturday, June 22, 2002, a day of fasting and prayer in spiritual preparation for the Solemn Assembly the following Saturday and the various ministries by youth groups throughout the week. The second day of gathering, the Solemn Assembly on June 29, 2002, featured prayer for the Youth of America and a special time of prayer for The Peace of Jerusalem. Eighty-five thousand people gathered.

The ministry that Dixie and her husband, Richard, had originally started, New York City Relief, has continued to grow, and growth brings greater responsibilities. Their outreach to the poor has expanded into New Jersey and more recently into Ethiopia. Dixie's passion for Africa is clearly revealed as she relates, "Richard has been traveling to Ethiopia for over ten years. Four years ago, friends of ours, a New York City pastor and his wife, felt led by God to return to their native land of Ethiopia. We have been able to support them as they have developed numerous areas of ministry in the city of Mekele in the northern region of Tigrai. One of the most exciting developments has been the building of an orphanage for some of the many homeless children in that region."

Her pace of explanation accelerated as she continued, "God has given us a recent burden after reading *Hospital by the River.* This book chronicles the special medical needs of the women in Ethiopia and the history of the establishing of this great work to treat obstetric fistula. On our last trip to Mekele, we worked to cut a path through the usual 'red tape' in hopes of establishing a way for short-term medical personnel to be of service there. They would be free to help with any medical needs they find, and we will help serve as liaison with the regional health department, hospital, and medical school. Though we have yet to take or send our first medical mission team, and this is a totally new area for us, believing we have heard from God, we must do our best."

Although ministry has called Dixie and her husband to Africa several times, their home base remains the New York City area. The courage and obedience to God that enabled her to help bring unity to the women in New York City have served her well in everyday life. Whether her family, church, or ministry responsibilities require her attention and energies, her defining characteristics remain—courage and obedience to God.

WHAT CAN ONE WOMAN DO?

WHAT CAN DIXIE, ONE WOMAN, DO?
Anything God wants to do through her!

WHAT CAN YOU DO?
Anything God wants to do through you!

CHAPTER SIX

A Witness From New York City— to Muslim Leaders

(VICKY MAHAIRAS)

"WHERE ARE YOU?

I WANT TO FIND YOU.

THESE PEOPLE TOLD ME

I WOULD FIND YOU

THROUGH THESE DRUGS.

WHERE ARE YOU?"

Her eyes—barely visible through the dangling strands of oily and uncombed hair—told the story. Vicky ran through Central Park in New York City grabbing one stranger after another, screaming the same question: "Who am I? Who am I?"

No one on that early summer day of 1968 tried to help this eighteen-year-old during her terrifying LSD experience. Only one older man stopped and said, "You are a beautiful young girl, please go home and get some rest." Others shoved her away and walked—almost ran—in the opposite direction.

No longer able to run, her chest burning from exhaustion and legs too weak to hold her, she crumbled to the ground, still crying, "Who am I?" She covered her eyes and her ears with her hands. She tried to shut out the terrifying vision of people trying to run from the flames. She cringed at the sounds of their screams from the pain. It had to be hell!

"Where are You, God?" she shouted. "I want to find You. These people told me I would find You through these drugs. Where are You? O God, if You get me through this day and let me live and keep my mind, I am going to find You—somehow!"

Vicky's rebellion, three months earlier, peaked when she had run away from home with only the clothes on her back and her rock-and-roll records. She fled to Central Park. It didn't take long before she encountered two hippies who had just come back from India. They claimed they had just met God through drugs. Vicky thought, *Oh, how wonderful! I am going to learn how to meditate and meet God and use my drugs to find Him.*

She moved into Greenwich Village with them and began smoking pot every day and taking LSD and using cocaine on the weekends. All seemed to be going so well until that bad LSD trip in Central Park and the flames of hell that made her cry out to God. What Vicky didn't realize was that God had heard her!

One week later, her mind began to sort out circumstances more logically, and she began to see things more clearly. The process for a major change in her life began—a change that would affect not only her but her boyfriend, Tom.

She, Tom, and their hippie friends planned to hitchhike to California. The night before their departure, they all took LSD except for Vicky. Sadly, one of Vicky's friends, the girl who had been to India, went berserk and tried to jump out the window to commit suicide. Vicky was so frightened that early the next morning she ran to a neighbor's place and asked to use their phone. Her fingers quickly dialed her parents' number, and a sensation of relief washed over her as she heard the familiar calm voice.

"Hello."

"Mom, I want to come home and finish high school."

"If you are willing to obey us, Vicky, we will take you back."

She returned home to finish high school, and Tom disappeared for a time. He had taken so many drugs he thought he was the incarnation of Jesus Christ, so his parents asked him to attend group therapy at Lenox Hill Hospital. He thought he was signing a paper for group therapy, but he was signing papers to put himself into a mental institution to receive ten shock treatments.

On his day of release from the hospital, Tom hitchhiked to the mountains to find peace and to get away from the city. As he was wandering around on a lonely street in a little town in upstate New York, a stranger about his age walked up to him and asked, "Have you ever thought about spiritual things?"

Tom thought he was Jesus Christ, so he said, "Yup."

The conversation went from subject to subject, and Tom was drawn to what he heard. He was fascinated that the stranger had a little black book with all the answers to his questions. He accepted an invitation to return with this young man to a beautiful camp in upper New York State to hear more about "who he [Tom] thought he was," *Jesus Christ*. At the Word of Life camp, he met Christ.

A week later, Vicky picked up the ringing telephone and listened as the familiar voice said, "Vicky, I have found an Island of Love! You must come up." She assumed it was a hippie commune, so she hitchhiked to this "Island of Love." There, she too learned about the personal God, Jesus Christ. But it was not through her drugs that she found Jesus—it was through prayer, just as Tom had met Him.

THE LIFE-CHANGING POWER OF JESUS CHRIST

Vicky and Tom discovered the astounding, life-changing power of Jesus Christ. The founder of Word of Life, Jack Wirtson, took them under his wing and became their spiritual coach. He called them just about every week of his life for as long as he lived and poured the love of God into their lives. They immediately began to live a celibate lifestyle, enrolled in a university where they could study the Scriptures, and upon graduation they married and moved back to New York City.

For over twenty-five years as pastors of a church just north of

Harlem in New York City, Tom and Vicky have been the catalysts to bring new life to multitudes of other searching people. Theirs has been a holistic ministry. They started a school to educate children from kindergarten through eighth grade, a drug rehabilitation program, a homeless ministry that has fed over one million people, and camps in upper New York. Presently, they are serving in a ministry to encourage and equip leaders around the world in the task of bringing others to the One who possesses "life-changing power."

The first time I met Vicky, at one of Dixie's monthly meetings for ministry leaders, I felt an immediate kinship. We responded to the same drumbeat. She told me of how she and her daughters had been touched at the first Women's Prayer Summit. They were eager for another one!

We had a vacuum to fill on our Executive Committee for the upcoming second prayer summit because Carol Vedral (see Chapter Ten) had informed me that their new ministry required her full time. I knew it would take a remarkable woman to replace Carol, and it didn't take long to recognize that Vicky was another remarkable woman. I immediately began to pray about Vicky and asked the Lord to prepare her heart. He blessed us with her yes when I called a few weeks later and asked her to join our Executive Committee.

Several years later, I discovered the wonder of what God had done that day. Vicky confided, "When you approached me that day, I had never attended one of those monthly Women in Leadership meetings that Dixie sponsored. However, that morning I felt led by God to go down to be with the women and be encouraged, and then you approached me right after that."

I never cease to be astonished at the way God works! I thought God was answering only our need, but He was also filling a void in Vicky's life.

"To me it was a gift from God in my life. My husband had just resigned from being the pastor of Manhattan Bible Church for twenty-five years. I had always been a pastor's wife, and that world had ceased abruptly for me. I felt as if I were somehow adrift. My husband was still traveling and ministering, but my role had decidedly changed. I thought, *God is so good to give me an opportunity to still be involved in the lives of women!* He has blessed me with His presence and His Word, and it is a torch that He has given us to pass on to other women. I was so thrilled that I could be a part of it."

What else helped Vicky be so receptive to becoming a vital part of the committee for our second prayer summit?

"God had changed the life of my oldest daughter through the first prayer summit. She had gone through a hard divorce—abandonment, brokenness, and bitterness had come into her life. It was through the prayer summit that God released her from bitterness and brought back the joy of the Lord into her life. About five years later, God provided her with a godly Christian man.

"At the first prayer summit, I sensed the awesome openness and availability of God's presence so much. I felt He wanted our prayer lives to increase even more. Things that were barriers in Christianity were broken down at that meeting. He was drawing Christians from every denomination. Because we went beyond our denominations, we were the Body of Christ. It was awesome to me. It was a touch from heaven about the power of prayer—

how committed we must be to pray about everything.

"That didn't stop at the prayer summit. I sensed that as I served on the Executive Committee. Whenever we talked about something, we would hear, 'Let's pray about it.' And that became a practice I incorporated into my life ever increasingly. When I am with women, when I am talking with them on the phone, wherever we are, I say, 'Let's stop and pray about it right now.' So God increased the level of prayer in my own life. I grasped the power of it, how it really does arrange and change the course of people's lives."

Vicky continued, "At the second prayer summit, God helped my youngest daughter. She was in her teens and came to the prayer summit with her friend, and they thought it was going to be a boring time. One woman stepped up to the podium, and my daughter thought, *Oh, what is this gray-haired lady going to say to us?* As the woman described her struggle with the lesbian lifestyle, my daughter was mesmerized by her testimony. She began weeping for her young friends who are so confused. She sensed the power of God and knew that God wanted to use her. Her life is fully committed to the Lord. Having raised her in the inner city, surrounded by many people who have a lot of problems, we are delighted she has turned out to be a beautiful Christian girl."

Vicky minored in Greek and is a gifted teacher. After an intense session of prayer at the second Women's Prayer Summit, God used her message about the "new life that Christ gives" to bring many women to accept the forgiveness of Christ. Some went home as new believers in Jesus, and others departed with a peace-filled mind after realizing He paid the absolute penalty for all their sins upon the cross.

FIVE YEARS AFTER THE PRAYER SUMMIT

"As God has shaped me, I have many executive and administrative skills. My husband's ministry, CitiVision, is a baby ministry. The other day I was sharing that I didn't feel so useful, and he said, 'Vicky, everything I do, I couldn't do without you. You truly are a co-laborer with me in the Gospel.' So, for about three years I did a lot of administrative work for CitiVision, building our relationships with people, as well as my involvements with home and ministry.

"With God's grace we have been able to build two beautiful camps, reaching church children between the ages of eight and eighteen. For instance, we gave nine-year-old Michael a scholarship to camp last summer, and when he came back, he said to my husband, 'Do you know the best thing about camp? I heard that Jesus loves me.'

"Our contact with Michael had begun at the Manhattan Bible Church's feeding program. Many years ago, while my husband was pastor, we went to our community planning board and asked how we could help. They told us there was a great need for food. So we began a ministry program where the people would come in every night between 4 and 6 P.M. They would sit down, and we served them their meals and shared the Gospel with them every night. We discovered the need for a food pantry for low-income people in our community, so we have added one. We have about one hundred and fifty families who come once a week to get their bags of food. We do a banquet every Christmas and provide a Christmas present for everyone who comes. And then we do the Angel Tree program, working with other churches in the city. We have about four hundred children in the Angel Tree.

"After Michael came back from camp, we gave him a scholarship to the Academy at Manhattan Bible Church. He walks to every church service by himself. Even on Wednesday nights, he comes, eats his dinner, comes to the Bible and prayer time for the children, and walks home alone. The best thing about this whole story is that his mother, just last week, became a believer in Jesus! It's amazing! Our church followed up on him, and his mom came to the Lord,

"We try to minister to these families on a long-term basis. We follow up on them, and many people have become followers of Christ through the homeless ministry. The program is funded through donations and then through the Food for Survival, a corporation here in New York City.

"As I mentioned, CitiVision is an international ministry that my husband, Tom, started, which motivates and equips people to share the Gospel. We travel from city to city as well as go to third-world cities. We have developed seminars on "Fishing"—learning how to fish for people. It covers how to clean your nets; how to mend your nets; how to cast your nets; and how to bring in a harvest for the Lord.

"We have been to Nigeria, southern India, and we frequently go to Greece. In Greece, we do a training session for young leadership from anywhere in Baltic areas, such as Kosovo and Scorpio. Last year we had four hundred and fifty young

Christian leaders. My husband and four other pastors provided the training. We have always believed in holistic ministry, and that is what CitiVision is all about—finding out what kind of bait the fish like. We teach, 'Find out what bait that person needs to come to Christ and use that, because we are shaped by God to influence people in our sphere.' We also teach that we don't have to have a pulpit to reach people. Every individual has been shaped by God with all these gifts and experiences to bring a basketful of fruit for the harvest. We are writing a book, *Extreme Faith,* to give to local churches to help them catch the spirit of evangelism.

"I have also done some women's retreats where I have taught the Word of God and the ministry of prayer, and I plan to do more.

"The greatest thing that God did in my prayer ministry was with my own sister, Judy. Because she was five years older than me, we had almost no relationship while we were growing up. From the time I became a Christian, we were never close. But God has brought me into her life, and she told me that I have become her best friend. She reads the Bible every day now and has put her hope and confidence in Him. God has radically changed my life with her, my family, and her children, which has been a big answer to prayer. It is incredible. We have bonded, and we are true sisters now.

"I realize that the people in my life are my sphere of influence. Although God took me out of the role of a pastor's wife, I still disciple women and am very involved in counseling women on a one-to-one basis.

"For years, I have worked in managing the resources for family members of a leader to thirty-five million Muslim people. Right now I have opportunities to share the Gospel with all the staff of my boss—the cooks, chef, chauffeurs, family members, and international family members whom I have visited and who have also come to visit me. Our chats are not limited to just five-minute time frames but are forty-five minutes to an hour, and I am able to pray for them. I simply ask, 'How may I pray for you?'

"And that is how I started out witnessing to 'His Highness,' the leader of thirty-five million Muslim people. We had worked on the finances for the family, and when he was ready to dismiss me, I said, 'Your Highness, I realize that you are in charge of thirty-five million people, and I would like to pray for you. I am sure you have some personal burdens. How may I pray for you?' That is how I started to share the Gospel with him. He asked me to sit down, and he told me that there is only one true God, and I said, 'Yes, I know that.' We both may have been thinking different things.

"I was able to share about ten scriptures about Jesus Christ and my personal testimony with him. At the end of the conversation, I said, 'Your Highness, I don't want to be offensive to you, but the Bible says, *There is no other name under heaven given among men whereby we can have salvation, that's the Name of Jesus and at His Name, one day every knee shall bow and confess that He is Lord* (Acts 4:12). After our talk, he sent me a letter, saying he had never had a conversation before with a Christian like me.

"I felt God in that room more than I had ever experienced in my life. I was able to share with this man, a ruler of over thirty-five million Muslim people."

A MESSAGE FOR TODAY'S WOMAN

In our interview, I asked Vicky to share what God has put on her heart for you, today's woman.

"Women in America struggle with so many issues, thinking that we have to strive. We strive to obtain some type of purpose by rising up the corporate ladder and to be paid equally as a man. My message to women is that we may have a greater fulfillment and abundant life than when we try to control our life. For me, the greatest message is in yielding, not just in committing. Because, when we commit, we still have control. For example, if I decide I am going to commit an hour to the Lord, I still have to do it. I may not keep my commitment. To me it is about surrender, realizing that I am a soldier in God's army, a farmer in His vineyard, and an athlete running the race.

"Not everybody is going to find that fulfilled life. There are people who claim to know Christ and don't live an abundant life. There are women who are working like crazy, working long hours, giving their children over to other people to raise them, trying to have a name and find fulfillment in their identity or in the things they perform. How ironic is it that God says that fulfillment comes to those who 'rest'? Fulfillment comes to the eagle that catches the wind, that doesn't keep flapping and flapping. Fulfillment comes to *those who wait upon God*, those who really enter into God's rest. Hebrews 4 says that unbelief keeps us from entering into His rest.

"For women of faith, which God calls us to be, it is not about our husband's faith or our children's faith. Our personal faith is what ignites the power of God in our life. It is what invigorates us to be fulfilled. It is a personal faith relationship with Jesus Christ. We have to dig deep. We can't get it from somebody else. We can go to a great church and listen to the best preachers on the radio, but we have to dig to have a personal private time with God, to enter into God's rest.

"God wants women to have contentment. I have entered into contentment in my life. I don't feel a striving spirit. I am not jealous of anyone. God is going to supply everything that I need. In Philippians 4, the apostle Paul says, *Not that I speak from expedia.* The Greek word there is *hysteria.* We don't have to speak from *hysteria.* He said, *Sometimes I have a lot in my life, and I know how to go through humble circumstances—not that I speak from want* (that's *hysteria* again). Christians who walk with God don't have to have *hysteria.* But God has given us a sound mind, not the spirit of fear.

"Too many of us have anxieties in our lives. We have discontentment. We are often frustrated because we don't have the marriage we thought we would have. Our children, into whom we poured our lives, have not turned out the way we planned. Nobody puts a price tag on our self-worth except Jesus Christ.

God taught me that many years ago—He has put a price tag on me. And I am the most valuable person in the world because of 'God in me' and what I mean to Him. And you are the most valuable person in the world because of 'God in you' and what you mean to Him.

"The scripture that God has given me is that which Jesus spoke to the Samaritan woman at the well, who was so thirsty. *Whoever drinks the water I give him will never thirst. Indeed, the water I give him will become in him a spring of water welling up to eternal life* (John 4:14). This is the abundant life that Christ promised us.

"Think of John 15, where Jesus states that we will bear fruit that remains, and we will have so much joy that we can't contain it. But it involves coming to the place where we let God clean our life up. He comes in, lifts us up, gets the sunlight into our life, rearranges things, and aerates us. Not only does He aerate us, but He uses those pruning shears. If you have ever been to a vineyard, you know that without pruning there is no fruit. The pruning is from such a loving hand. God is *the true vinedresser.* There is no way to bring forth the grapes without it. I thank God for His loving character.

"Look at the Canaanite woman who went to Jesus for her demon-possessed daughter in Matthew 15:21–28. Jesus at first doesn't even answer her; then He tells her He only came for Jewish people. Finally, He invalidates her, suggesting that to help her would be like taking the children's bread and tossing it to their dogs. But this woman had such a great faith that she would not let go of the love of God, even though He seemed to be pushing her away. God often pushes us into difficult circumstances so that we can come to know Him as someone who really loves us. He has the best for us.

"When we are first giving our life to God, we tend to be afraid of what He is going to do to us. But when we know His character and love, we can answer in faith, 'Lord, You promised.' The Canaanite woman said to Jesus, 'Yes, Lord, but even the dogs eat the crumbs from their masters' table,' and He granted her request because of her great faith. We have to answer God in faith even when it doesn't look as though God is doing what we want Him to do.

"It is so awesome to have extreme faith, to live a life where we pray every day for every need we have. That's the kind of God we have, where we can cry out to women all over the world, even in the countries where they are persecuted. It is awesome how great God is!"

God did not abandon Vicky in Central Park in New York City when she searched for Him, and God will not abandon you! You may, confidently, say with Vicky: *For you, O Lord, have never abandoned anyone who searches for you* (Psalms 9:10 *New Living Translation*).

VICKY "DID IT AFRAID"

As I talked with Vicky to update this chapter three and one-half years later, she was sitting at a desk that overlooks Central Park, looking down upon the very place where she had cried out in desperation to Jesus Christ, thirty-nine years earlier. As she pondered the wonder of it all, she quoted Habakkuk 3:2: *LORD, I have heard of your fame; I stand in awe of your deeds, O LORD.*

In the last couple of years, she has accompanied her husband on international crusades to Paraguay and Uganda. She shared how she became fearful as the trips approached, so one morning she dropped to her knees and had a long talk with God about it. After she had finished praying, she got up and turned on the television. The first words she heard were "Do it afraid!"

Talk about an immediate answer to prayer! That caught Vicky's attention. The well-known biblical teacher went on to explain that many times she had been fearful when she felt the Lord was telling her to do something, and as she had dialogued (argued) with God, she heard *that still small voice* saying, "Do it afraid!"

Certainly, in this world there are many situations about which one can be fearful. In Gulu, Uganda, Vicky learned of ten Internally Displaced People Camps (IDPC). Each camp has from twenty to thirty thousand people in it. The camps have no sanitation or fresh water, even though they are close to the beautiful fresh water of the Nile. The cows and the people drink from and bathe in the same filthy source of water. Vicky is raising funds and researching the best way to get fresh water into the camp. She is beginning with one camp, but is she praying that each camp will soon have a supply of clean fresh water.

In Campala, Uganda, she and her husband held Abstinence Pride Crusades, attended by thirty-five thousand college students. Five thousand students meet together each week to uphold and encourage one another to take pride in their commitment of sexual abstinence before marriage and faithfulness to one partner in marriage. A moral stand as this requires courage in a culture where such a lifestyle is viewed unfavorably and even ridiculed.

In addition to her work, Vicky continues to mentor the

women at the church they founded, Manhattan Bible, located in the most northern corner on Manhattan. As an update, Michael is now a teenager and still attends Manhattan Bible. Pray for this young man. Who knows what God has planned for his life?

Vicky and Tom have eight grandchildren, and she has been struck with the necessity of passing her faith on to them, so that they will look back and exclaim with her to all the world, *Lord, I have heard of your fame, I stand in awe of your deeds.*

So, once again we ask, what can one woman do?

WHAT CAN VICKY DO? WE ANSWER,
Anything God wants to do through her.

AND WE ALSO ASK, WHAT CAN YOU DO? WE ANSWER,
Anything God wants to do through you.

CHAPTER SEVEN

Prepared and Positioned for Ministry Following 9/11

(Joyce Mattera)

"WE TARGETED THE MOST

GANG-RIDDEN, DRUG-INFESTED,

VIOLENT STREETS OF THE

NEIGHBORHOOD IN BROOKLYN.

THERE WERE CONSTANT GUN

BATTLES. I WILL NEVER FORGET

THE DAY I SAW A SIXTEEN-YEAR-OLD

BOY KILLED IN A GUN BATTLE

WITH THE POLICE. WE PRAYER-

WALKED THOSE BLOCKS IN 1980."

When Joyce was growing up in Brooklyn between the ages of eleven and fifteen, one would never have predicted that one day she would prayer-walk the most violent streets in Brooklyn. But those were the days before she met Jesus! During those years, her life was taking a decidedly different path. She began to use drugs and proceeded to sell them. She said, "I was miserable, always having to lie, always having to sneak around." At the age of fifteen, to her great relief, her parents discovered what she was doing.

Joyce said, "God sent a girl from my crowd to talk to me. She had been raised in a family of faith but had turned away to run with the rest of us. We noticed a change in her when she began attending her church again. She began to live differently and tried to explain the reason to us. She said, 'Jesus has become real in my life.' As she prayed, the Lord laid on her heart the names of two people to whom she was to talk.

"I was one of those people. She didn't want to approach me because I made fun of her new lifestyle, but she decided to obey God. One day she took me aside and began to share her faith with me. I knew, without a doubt, that she was speaking truth, and that I needed to make my life right. Even though I did not understand what she meant, I wanted to have peace with God, but I was haunted by the question, 'How?'

"She invited me to her church, and four weeks later, I discovered the answer! After the church service, the speaker asked if anyone would like to 'Come to Jesus.' He invited us to come to the front of the church and said someone would pray with us. It seemed too simple. Could this unrest within me be obliterated by praying with someone, to someone? Nevertheless, I went up and simply asked Christ to be real in my life in the same manner I saw that He was real in the lives of others. That night my life changed, and from that point on, I wanted to serve God with all my heart."

God had a plan for Joyce. Not only was His plan perfect, so was His timing. As she pursued her new life as a follower of Christ, she became involved in smaller groups of believers, where she eventually met a young man who stood out from everyone else. He had become a believer when he was nineteen and had entered Bible school. At the time of their meeting, he had recently returned from a very dangerous mission trip to Turkey, which was under martial law, and he had a heart for reaching the world. They began ministering together, doing drama and puppet shows in Brooklyn. Their friendship matured into love and marriage.

Their honeymoon, though, was not your ordinary, everyday dream trip. It was 1980, during the Cold War days with the Soviet Union, and they went on a short-term mission trip—smuggling Bibles to believers in Russia. Joyce describes it this way: "We had two months of dodging KGB officers. It was fun. In one city we were caught, and the officials tried to set us up with black marketing to get us imprisoned. What an experience!

"We had planned to come back from our honeymoon and go into business. But when we came back home, the contrast between the closed Soviet Union and the freedom to preach openly in Brooklyn was too great an opportunity to pass up. We could not walk away from it. We felt God's call to start a church instead of going into business."

TRANSFORMING NEIGHBORHOODS

"We shared God's call upon our lives with our pastor, and he released us with his blessing and oversight. We began our work with four other people: my husband's parents, his best friend, and his best friend's wife. Soon others joined us.

"I quickly became aware of the plight of the children in the community we were evangelizing. In my outreach to children and youth, we targeted the worst blocks in the neighborhood—Forty-Ninth, Sixtieth, and Sixty-First Streets. This was a very low-income area with many challenges. Most families with whom we connected were broken and dysfunctional. Gangs and drugs were rampant. Children were left to fend for themselves in conditions unfit for living. Gun battles were nothing unusual. Etched forever in my brain is the vivid image of watching as a sixteen-year-old boy was shot and killed in a gun battle with the police as I walked down the street. Forty-Ninth Street was so bad it would be closed for months at a time. Our car windows even had bullet holes in them.

"The suffering children—we were so burdened for them! We began by walking the streets and praying for the people. Every night we set up equipment and started giving puppet shows and skits. The kids began to come out. They were vulnerable and at-risk but very responsive to help. We built up a large children's outreach, even before my husband officially started the church. We picked up the children and brought them to whatever building we could rent. Sometimes we discovered the parents had left them home alone all weekend, so we had to get them dressed and fed. There were times when the parents had simply left, so the Bureau of Child Services took them.

"For years we picked up the children weekly and brought them to a program designed to deter them from following the same destructive lifestyles that surrounded them. At one point, we were only able to operate this outreach once a month, but we began visiting the homes of these children on a regular basis. My burden and cry was that we were not doing enough. The needs were so great! It was as if we were trying to close a gaping wound with a Band-Aid.

"There was so much more I wanted to do; there was so much more they needed. I longed for a more holistic program so we could more effectively help the children and their families in a real way. I wanted to have programs to meet the needs of foster care, counseling, tutoring, language skills, and job support— programs to counteract teenage pregnancies and fatherless children and much more.

"Little by little, the parents from one particular block started attending our church and other local churches after accepting Christ as their Lord. Changes began to take place. That pattern continued, and today that block has a large number of Christian families. They are continuing to reach out in a positive way to this community.

"One of the families that came to the Lord because we picked up their children caught the vision. The mother, herself, has taken in foster children from drug-addicted parents five different times. She helped the parents get into rehabilitation programs, and while they were in treatment, she cared for their children. Through her example of loving concern, many families received help and were reunited."

INTIMACY WITH THE DIVINE

I did not meet Joyce at our Brooklyn Focus Group, but her husband attended. As he heard about the vision of the Women's Prayer Summit in The Theater At Madison Square Garden, he was reminded of his wife's prayer of some years earlier. They had attended a small prayer group in Manhattan close to Madison Square Garden. During the course of that evening, Joyce had looked up, pointed to the Garden, and said, "That is where we need to be praying." She had then prayed, "Lord, please fill it with your praying servants." He suggested we might be interested in her ministry, and we were.

I learned that Joyce's primary ministry was *private prayer*. I loved to listen to her pray. Before speaking, she would have a period of silence, as if she were preparing to approach her Lord, and then she would begin, barely above a whisper, to declare her love and devotion to her great confidante, the Lord of lords and King of kings, Jesus Christ. From there she would petition Him with such fervency that one could not doubt being in the presence of the divine. It was this type of prayer relationship, this intimacy with God, that enabled her to serve on our Executive Committee.

Almost immediately after joining, she discovered she was pregnant. This presented a real problem! She said, "During my four previous pregnancies, I had been very sick, every day for nine months. I moved from the couch, to the bathroom, back to bed. I thought, *How can I be pregnant now?* It did not make sense. When I am pregnant, I can't work, can't function, and can't get up from the bed.

"I remembered that I had always experienced a two-week window before I became nauseated, so I vowed to pray during that time. Early every morning for two weeks, I went to my special prayer spot near the shoreline in South Brooklyn. There is a park and a walkway along the waterfront. It has a fabulous view of the whole Manhattan skyline. It was very quiet, almost deserted at that time of day. Each day I spent at least two hours in solitude with the Lord, praying, believing! I knew that I had to believe God before my nausea began. I prayed and prayed, and then I simply began to thank God, believing that He was going to enable me to function. In fact, I did not ask anyone else to pray with me about it until I had the assurance in my heart that He had answered. At that time, I went to my church and asked them to thank God with me. And I never got sick! So I was able to continue to do everything that I needed to do."

Joyce led our ticket sales teams with Dixie for the first prayer summit, spoke and prayed in all six of the mini-prayer summits and preliminary meetings for women ministry leaders, and spoke and prayed at both Women's Prayer Summits. As an Executive Committee member, she took care of other tasks too numerous to list. She also served as a corporate board member of the Women's Prayer Summit, Inc.

She continued, "Before I heard about the prayer summit, God prepared me to release some responsibilities and free up my schedule because He had a special assignment for me. When I became a committee member of the Women's Prayer Summit, I had to resign from many previous responsibilities. Our church purchased a large building to renovate into a church, and I was not even able to be involved in it. I also asked others to assume my leadership of the children's ministry. I knew this commitment would require a great deal of my time, so I asked my family for their blessing. If they had resented the time it was going to take, I would have declined. I had four children, and I found my biggest challenge was scheduling care for them when I needed to be away."

THE POWER OF UNITED CORPORATE PRAYER

"I have always believed strongly in prayer and especially in corporate prayer—united prayer of the Body of Christ in a city or region. I had heard testimonies from different places where people had gathered for united prayer, and God had changed the spiritual climate of their area. I had long desired to have this in my city.

"When I heard about the Women's Prayer Summit, I knew it was from God, and I wanted to be part of it. I wanted to do whatever I could to see it happen. When I was asked to join the Executive Committee, I knew this was what God had been preparing me for.

"The women of our committee were from very different backgrounds, which I found to not be a challenge but to be something very powerful. It helped me—helped all of us—to grow. I enjoyed that. I had known some of the women by name but had never met them. This endeavor afforded me the opportunity to establish relationships with women of God, strong relationships that I still have today.

"I was already of the mind-set that we needed to work together as the Body of Christ, recognizing our differences and still working together, and see how God would mesh us 'as one voice' so that we could be more effective. The Women's Prayer Summit was the greatest picture and example of different backgrounds—denominational, socio-economic, and cultural—all coming together. I had never seen that attempted and succeed elsewhere to this degree.

"I know it was because we had a committee of different backgrounds and because we decided that we were going to work through all our differences as a committee. God enabled us to channel this mind-set down to everyone with whom we associated and right into the big day at the Garden, where women gathered as one from every denomination, ethnicity, and social background. That was one of the most powerful manifestations. Women at the prayer summit all shared that belief. It showed that it could be done. Together, we could do it!

"In order for this to happen, it takes strong secure leadership—someone who has the openness for people of different backgrounds to work in concert, who is not threatened by that, who does not insist on 'only my way.' It stems from a committee working together, that mind-set and blessing overflowing to all the spheres of influence of the committee members. It was a great inspiration to me.

"The unseen power behind all this was prayer. Prayer behind the scenes makes things happen. It sets the stage. I have seen this in the building of our church and in our work. Prayer was crucial, first of all, to make the Women's Prayer Summit happen, and then to make it succeed.

"The day following the prayer summit, I really felt the spiritual atmosphere had been affected by our prayers. The issues that we tackled and prayed specifically about are key issues that the enemy is trying to use to destroy families and our nation. You can see that from what has been happening and what is going on. I believe our prayers, without even seeing the plans the enemy had, were prophetic and on target. Who knows the full effect of those prayers? But I know that needs not to be an end-all—only a catalyst to keep us praying, and calling the church to pray for these issues that are attacking our families and our nation for generations to come. So I think we heard from the heart of God for that which we needed to pray.

"In a practical sense, the prayer summit helped me to step out further. It equipped me to develop areas of my life that I previously had not allowed. It enabled me not only to know that I could do this, but that *I could do it!* That kind of faith has catapulted me into being able to serve God in greater strength and to develop other giftings in my life.

"In the past, fear of failure had often kept me from taking on challenges. Working in the prayer summit really helped me get beyond that. After the summit, I could take on projects without fear of failure. That was a personal accomplishment in my life."

PREPARED FOR 9/11 MINISTRY

"Following the second prayer summit, I was at home, caring for and home schooling my children and seeking God. I had not planned to reassume the leadership of the children's outreach in our community. As it turned out, the people who were running it had to step out, so I had no choice.

"I had to change gears. This new responsibility required my full time. In the past I had envisioned many needs but had never attempted them. Now, I said, 'Okay, God, You called me back, so I am going to seek out the funding to support this work and to add the programs we have needed for so long.' I began the work, but we needed additional support. Our church helped but could not carry the whole financial load.

"The children's community outreach was large and consuming. We reached about two thousand children. Each month we actually visited about one thousand kids and picked them up and brought them to the program. We had a volunteer staff of about fifty, and occasionally a few more helped. It was very hard to run this huge operation with volunteers. I actually said I was going to put it on hold for a little while, but then 9/11 struck, and we said, 'No, we have to pull the whole thing together.' God opened doors for us.

"After 9/11, we were even more burdened for our neighborhood. Our unobstructed view of the Manhattan skyline meant that as our children looked out the windows of their schools and the park in this community, they watched the Twin Towers burn and fall to the ground. Some were orphaned when parents and single mothers perished in the Trade Center. A lot of strong members in the community were lost. As you would expect, the children were very traumatized. Some were affected so severely that they would not go back to school or even leave their homes.

"World Vision came into the city after 9/11 and funded organizations doing trauma relief. Because we had such a large base and they knew us, we were positioned to work with them. They funded an administrator and a full-time counselor and supplied a trailer for us. I said, 'Okay, God, you are opening the door, so I will have to keep carrying this through.' That funding was temporary, lasting for only eight months.

"But God provided. The Robin Hood Foundation heard

about us and liked what we were doing. They said, 'Hire more counselors.' Later, they increased their funding and told us to hire more counselors. So we hired five full-time counselors.

"When our counselors went into the homes to counsel families impacted by the events of 9/11, they found appalling situations. Their visits revealed broken homes, drug addiction, and neglected children. We addressed their circumstances with counseling and resources. Finally, we were able to provide the assistance of which I had always dreamed!

"Our counselors are bilingual. The predominant language of the families with whom we are working is Spanish. They are from many Hispanic backgrounds. We also have many Asians and Arabs. They come to our sessions because we help them and bring healing. I believe that we relieved a lot of tension after 9/11 by just working with them. We have since been able to extend our programs to include workshops for the parents. The name of our organization is Children of the City.

"For as long as I have been working in this neighborhood, I have dreamed of being able to rescue the children out of homes where abuse and neglect abound. We now have a guardianship program. We look for loving homes where these children may live while we help the parents.

"We are currently taking in children. The parents have given us legal guardianship. When staff from different government agencies come to their homes, they tend to hide, but they will work with us, because they trust us. We have been a solid presence in the neighborhood since 1981, so people know us. They ask, 'Will you please take my kids?' Even before a formal foster care agency could be established, some gave us guardianship so they could enter a drug rehabilitation program.

"We have been able to start a very successful after-school program. We developed it to address the overwhelming academic deficiencies and drop-out rates in the area. We are seeing huge increases in children's reading levels, and we are working with the kids and helping them on a more continual basis. We bring in some of the children, preteens, and teens and talk out all the issues they have to face, including sexual abuse.

"They come here throughout the week for numerous meetings and get help to stay in school. It is difficult. The public school curriculum is geared for parents who have an academic background sufficient to be able to help their children. The problem, however, is that many of the parents of the children in our program do not speak English. Consequently, they are unable to help their children. The system is hard for inner-city culture, but we are working to overcome that. In our after-school program, we are also going to be working with the parents and enabling them to be able to help their children.

"It is so rewarding to see kids who would have dropped out of high school now graduating and even going on to college. We support a young man who has been living with us, and he will soon graduate from college. It gives us a wonderful sense of satisfaction.

"The neighborhood has changed so much that we seldom see gang activity. What a change from the days when we first walked the neighborhood and found ourselves stuck in hallways, dodging bullets between gang fights. Thank God, we don't have any of that now. Instead, we have seen the lives of gang leaders and drug dealers turned around.

"In fact, one of our youth directors, who is also a professional value-based 'rapper,' was one of the first kids we picked up. Now he is married, has a family and home. One of our van drivers was the first gang member we worked with. The former head of the Latin Kings in the neighborhood, who was brought up with a mother on drugs and a father in jail, gave his life to the Lord and was so transformed I failed to recognize him. He had cut his hair, has his own business, is in college, and is helping with the youth. These are just some of the testimonies that are so powerful. It is gratifying to see the people stay in the neighborhood and pour back into it.

"We have seen people once on welfare who now have their own businesses and own their own homes. We are trying to break the destructive cycles associated with poverty and welfare. We help them initially, but we try to break the welfare mentality. We teach that when they live like that they stay poor. We say, 'Look, this is not where you want to stay.' So we have been able to see change."

AFFECTING THE CULTURE FOR CHRIST

As I went to interview Joyce, I parked in front of a beautiful yellow Brooklyn church and walked safely inside to meet her. I didn't fear flying bullets. The church stands as a testament to God's faithfulness. As we were ending our talk, I had to ask her one more question. "Joyce, where do you see yourself five years from now?"

"One of my husband's great callings in ministry is to affect the culture. That is also my calling. It has been our calling since we began together. Our oldest son has been taking a stand since his college days. He is in the national news and on radio because of the stand he is taking in culture.

"Networking with other churches and other pastors' wives and leaders is vital. That's what I loved about the prayer summit. My husband does that. Our relationships formed during the prayer summit have continued to grow. We still work together, do things together.

"The Pastor's Prayer Summit has also grown; they still meet. It is setting the stage for us to see God move in our city. I want to see God move in my city.

"I am not going anywhere. I believe that my city is going to be an influence for the Gospel in the world. Some people gloom and doom over their city, but I don't believe that. Our churches are praying. Our church is a strong praying church. We meet corporately on Tuesday nights and in groups during the week. We pray for our city and for our nation. We believe God is going to move mightily in our city. That is my heart, my desire.

"I know that without prayer we accomplish nothing of eternal value. We are praying and standing firm, working together because we know unity is another key factor. We see that happening more and more. It is so exciting to see so many of the key leaders of our city working together, and we know that is why we are going to be able to see success for the Lord.

"God wants to work in my city. I want to continue to build not only a strong church but a network together with other pastors and leaders in the city where no one person can do it or take cred-it for it. Then I want to work in my community with what God is building up as an example of what the church should be doing. This happens when we are not contained in our four walls, but when we are out influencing and serving our community.

"On every level, I want to continue to grow, to work with my children and see them and their children grow. We are not just living for today. Our goal is to train our young people and hand the work down to them so they may continue the work of God."

MINISTERING THROUGH THE PAIN

Before we closed our interview, I asked Joyce, "I know you have been working with children, but do you have a word for God's women?"

"On a personal level, even during the time of the prayer summit, there were personal struggles I had. Maybe it was my thorn in the flesh, but nevertheless the Lord has used the pain to work deeper in my own life and character.

"The year of 2003 was the hardest year of my life. I compared it to my first pregnancy, where I was so sick. After I gave birth, I remember thinking, *What is this weird feeling?* I felt good! I had become so accustomed to feeling physically sick that I didn't know what it was like not to be nauseated. It was nonstop—nine months, twenty-four hours a day. What I have realized during this time is that the emotional pain has been constant in that same way. I have not been without emotional pain, but I have found solace in the knowledge that God is faithful and that He has an end to all things. Now, when I minister in the pain and press on through the pain, I see an anointing in my life in ways I could never have imagined. It is not only when I minister to the children or others, but it is in everything. God worked so deeply in my life. In years to come, I expect to be able to give powerful testimony of God's work.

"There were times when I called my praying women to my house to pray for me because I felt I couldn't battle the difficulties myself. As a leader, I must let people know that I need their prayers. These times of prayer carried me over things I could not have battled on my own, so I do not hesitate to ask for prayer.

"I love ministering to women, and most of my teaching ministry has been for women. I teach out of the depth of my own experience. I see that women need self-esteem—confidence of who they are. Many women are apt to be downtrodden or oppressed naturally and spiritually. I want them to know that they can be used of God regardless of what has happened in their lives. God can use the most difficult things in their lives for good. I know the devil has a strategy, but God can turn that around and use it against the kingdom of darkness and bring good from it.

"Never give up; never, never give up; and know that God wants to use you! The only thing that can stop you is unbelief. If you do not believe something, you do not go for it. Be encouraged. God has a plan to use you. Do not underestimate your value. God does not!"

WHAT CAN ONE WOMAN DO? WE KNOW THE ANSWER:
Anything God wants to do through her!

WHAT CAN YOU DO?
Anything God wants to do through you!

CHAPTER EIGHT

From College Students to Global Christian Leaders

(BETZI SCHROEDER)

"I AM AN OPEN BOOK!

FOR AS LONG AS I CAN REMEMBER,

MY HEART'S DESIRE HAS BEEN

TO SERVE GOD."

A youthful dream and a servant's heart—this may be your prayer for your child or children. Perhaps you are asking, "How can one instill such a desire in a child?" I was also curious, so I asked Betzi, an Executive Committee member for our second prayer summit, to tell me about her life. I found some clues!

Betzi was born as the fifth child in a family of six children. Her parents met on a dance floor in New York City. The initial attraction they mutually felt for each another turned into a bond when they discovered the other had also emigrated from Germany. Love quickly grew, and marriage followed. Religion had played no significant role in either of their lives, and that did not change when they married.

Marriage presented new challenges. They found themselves working day and night to try to keep their newly established contracting business and growing family afloat. By the time three children had arrived, they were under stress. Then a radical change occurred in their lives.

They heard the concept of a "personal God in Jesus Christ." Investigation led them to a church, where they heard who Jesus was. When they heard what He did for them and offered them, they were enthralled and responded in faith!

Suddenly, everything changed. Certainly, they still encountered pressures, but they no longer faced them alone. The Spirit of God, who came to live within them when they confessed their sins and asked Christ to be their Redeemer, *set them free* (Romans 8:1) *and strengthened them with power to know the love of Christ that surpasses knowledge* (Ephesians 3:14–20). Through prayer and the living Scriptures, the Spirit of God provided a daily personal relationship with their great High Priest, Jesus (Hebrews 4:12–16).

They could not suppress the joy of their newfound faith, sharing it openly so that others could have the same fellowship with God. Their home became a sanctuary for others who were also new to this country. Betzi grew up in a household with an open door. Her mother lived by the creed: "Unexpected guests? Just add more water to the pot of soup!" The family table often seemed to expand as they squeezed closer together to make room for guests. Betzi recalls lively table conversations and captivating moments when special missionary guests told of adventures in far-off lands.

This was Betzi's life. The nurturing tools of family, church, and summer and winter camp experiences led her to an unmistakable personal commitment to Christ at the age of thirteen.

Her teen years, in Nyack, New York, were somewhat sheltered. A brother, two years older, kept a close eye out for his *younger sis* and often steered undeserving suitors (in his opinion) away. She enjoyed both security and a close sibling bond that would make most young girls envious.

However, when she was seventeen, one young man found a way to breach the barriers. As Betzi prepared to walk home after church one Sunday morning, she found herself face to face with a handsome young man, but she had no idea who he was.

Impulsively, he said, "I saw you in the choir this morning. Would you like a ride home?"

"No, thank you. I don't believe we have been introduced."

He persisted! The next week a friend at church approached her. At his side was the guy who had asked to drive her home.

"Betzi, I want you to meet my friend, David Schroeder. He is a freshman at Nyack." David's perseverance paid off.

Betzi graduated from high school and enrolled in Nyack, and the relationship flourished with her brother's approval! At the end of her sophomore year, there was no turning back. Her desire to serve the Lord was matched by this young man, and she agreed to become Mrs. David Schroeder.

APPRENTICESHIP REQUIRES FLEXIBILITY AND EXTENSIVE TRAINING

David had one more year before graduation, so Betzi exchanged school days for gainful employment. Each morning, as David went off to school, she headed into New York City to work as a data processor in the finance department at the Christian and Missionary Alliance in Times Square.

Upon graduation in 1968, the newlyweds made their way to Roseville, Minnesota, for seminary. At the conclusion of the first year, they learned that David's father was experiencing health problems. He asked David to come back to Harrisburg, Pennsylvania, to help in a Christian publishing business.

Two miracles and three short years in Pennsylvania proved to be providential. One miracle changed their lifestyle forever—a baby girl was born. The other opened the door for them to move on with their lives—David's father was miraculously healed. His doctor said, "I have no reason to explain this."

A call from Hillside Church in Armonk, New York, took them to prestigious Westchester County, where David served as the youth pastor. When the senior pastor left, he was asked to take that position. The people of the church welcomed them, and ministry was smooth sailing! Here they found lasting friendships. Betzi's days and nights were filled with the various roles of a young wife, mother (two baby boys joined their sister), and first lady of the church. She loved them all.

From Armonk, New York, this young family answered the call to move to Chatham, New Jersey, to serve under a seasoned and desirable mentor, Dr. Paul Bubna. David's apprentice role drastically changed when the pastor suffered a near fatal heart attack and required bypass surgery. David stepped up and filled the pulpit each week, preaching for a church membership of twelve hundred people. It was great training, and he soon felt comfortable with the large congregation. He continued until Dr. Bubna was able to reassume his preaching responsibilities.

At the first missionary conference after Dr. Bubna's return, Betzi and David attended different services. On the way home from church, there was silence. Both were deep in thought about what had occurred in the service.

Finally, David broke the ice. "Betzi, this morning during church, I distinctly felt God calling us for overseas mission work."

"The same thing happened to me, David."

When they compared notes, they knew God was calling them on. But Dr. Bubna was just getting back to work. Did God want them to leave now? Courage to make a much dreaded appointment did not come easily. David sat across from Dr. Bubna and once again learned from his mentor. "God's faithful giant" made the conversation much less painful.

"If God is calling you, I don't want to ever hold you back."

FROM AFFLUENCE TO A CONVERTED CHICKEN COOP AND BACK AGAIN

It has been said that God desires "servants who are comfortable drinking from a scooped out gourd or a crystal goblet, who are willing to wear hand-me-outs from the missionary bin or garments of fine silk, who love and honor poor illiterate individuals or highly educated and refined parishioners—all for the glory of God."

The call to Wokingham, England, required adjustment, to be sure. The initial call was to mentor eight young men preaching in home cell groups. However, Betzi and David ended up planting a church in Binfield, near London. Home in Binfield was a one-room, one-bath, converted chicken coop. To make the situation more inconvenient, it also served as their church sanctuary.

Each Sunday they pushed their beds into the bathroom and put out chairs for seventeen people—their own family of five, another family of five, and seven others. As the church grew, they were eventually able to move services to a school auditorium. The Schroeder family upgraded from the converted chicken coop to a delightful old English home with a garden, fishing pond, and a playhouse for the children. Both living and worship environments greatly improved.

A new experience of worship began to sweep across England while Betzi and David were there. Denominational barriers came down as people from Anglican, Brethren, Baptist, Catholic, and other churches began meeting together in house groups. Their worship consisted of an abundance of praise and prayer. The Holy Spirit united their hearts together in the Name of *Jesus*.

This was Betzi's first exposure to such a spirited worship attitude, and she found it a bit threatening at first. She began to sense, however, that it was a solid intimate walk with God that led to this display of affection toward Him. The Holy Spirit began to remove her resistance.

Was this what God wanted Betzi and David to learn while in England? Or was He testing their hearts? Would they serve Him as energetically while living and worshiping in a one-room converted chicken coop as they had in the affluent New York City suburban areas? Or was it simply that their work in England was completed? We can only speculate. However, whatever God's purpose, they must have passed the test. He made it perfectly clear that the time had come to return to the United States.

By the time the family of five Americans moved back to Chatham, New Jersey, the little church of seventeen had grown to forty people. It was hard to leave beloved believers who had become family to them. However, a missionary's work is to make disciples, and they could say, "Mission Accomplished."

The house back in Chatham, rented during their absence, became home once again. Betzi became a group leader at Bible Study Fellowship, and for the next five years David worked with Trans World Radio, a global mission organization.

Apprenticeship—where does it lead and when does it end? It led from Chatham, New Jersey, to Wolfeboro, New Hampshire, for one and one-half years.

"Actually," Betzi said, "we viewed this as our first sabbatical. We both worked at odd jobs and experienced God's provision in

some interesting ways. We sold our house in Chatham and purchased an old house that had been built in the 1800s—the Lucas
Noel House. It had been gutted and made into a bed-and-break-
fast but had never passed inspection for the certificate of occu-
pancy. We had to install five bathrooms. Our heat came from
three wood burning stoves, and in one winter we burned eight
cords of wood. Our kids still complain that the old house got so
cold during the night that ice formed on any water sitting out.

"Our mortgage payment source was even more unusual.
When we lived in Chatham, David had purchased an old
Mercedes from a colleague at work who restored old cars. While
in New Hampshire, the old car was like driving a tank in the
midst of snowstorms. All we had to do was aim it, and it got us
there. However, our financial situation called for more frugality.
Two cars were definitely a luxury, so we put it up for sale. The
buyer was unable to pay in one lump sum, so we worked out a
payment plan. The money we received from him each month
exactly paid our mortgage.

"David received some compensation from preaching at a
church in Wellesley, Massachusetts, but the schedule was grue-
some! Every Saturday we loaded the car with everything the
whole family needed while away from home and made the long
trek to Wellesley. After Sunday services, I drove back home with
the children, and David would stay to work nearby. He returned
back home on Thursday, and on Saturday the routine began all
over again. It was obvious this could not continue indefinitely.
When David received a call to become the President of the
Reformed Episcopal Seminary in the Philadelphia area, we

accepted. The seminary's name was later changed to Philadelphia Theological Seminary."

"MOM SCHROEDER"

After the family settled in Pennsylvania, Betzi accepted full-time employment with a pharmaceutical company. She also took advantage of nearby Eastern University at St. Davids, Pennsylvania, and completed her bachelor's degree in Organizational Management.

One day a local pastor approached David and said, "Please help me find Christian homes for seven children. Their father is a pedophile and is guilty of unspeakable atrocities to the children."

They were able to place six children but could find no one to take the most difficult child. No family felt qualified to handle an uncontrollable, angry, cursing, and street-wise eight-year-old girl who had been sexually abused.

David approached Betzi with the problem and suggested that they give Chelsia a home. A family conference produced division. Betzi was working full time, taking a full load at the university, and their twenty-year-old daughter had just moved back home. Her hands were full! She had no energy or enthusiasm for added responsibilities, particularly a troubled and uncontrollable child.

Betzi and one son voted no. David, their daughter, and the other son voted yes. The yes voters argued, "If we are against abortion, then we must be willing to step up to the plate to help, or we are hypocrites."

Betzi said, "Of course, I did not want to be a hypocrite! So I acquiesced. But it was not a good decision for me. I deeply resented being forced into this decision through guilt. The child threw our home into chaos with tantrums, screaming, nightmares, and sleeplessness. Our hands were tied by the foster care system as to how we responded to her. David and I switched roles, and my daughter and I switched roles. They nurtured her, and I resented her. I was jealous of the time and energy she took from David that I felt belonged to me when I was in need of it." Despite a divided family reception and Betzi's resentment, Chelsia finally began to make progress.

A year later, David was asked to become the Director of Higher Education for the Christian Missionary Alliance in Colorado Springs, Colorado. The family prepared to move, but what about Chelsia? State laws prohibited her from going along. The Schroeders were able to locate another Christian family in southeastern Pennsylvania who agreed to take Chelsia into their home. In spite of David's and Betzi's inner turmoil, Chelsia had experienced the love of a family who modeled loving relationships. When she left the Schroeders for her new home, she was skipping and praising God because of the internal joy she possessed because of Jesus. She did, however, remain an unresolved issue with Betzi for many years.

In Colorado Springs, Betzi began to put her degree to work. She served as an administrative assistant to a well-known Christian radio personality with a "focus upon the family." One thing in particular impressed her. The importance of every single person and every question was front and center to the founder. Consequently, he built accountability into the organizational operating procedures to assure this happened. It also made Betzi's job very interesting.

Fortunately, Betzi kept a loose grip upon "things." Soon, their house in Colorado Springs and the job she enjoyed would be in her past. David received an offer to become the president of a Christian college back in her hometown of Nyack, New York. She came back home, but not in the same role as many of the townspeople remembered her, the daughter of immigrants. She returned as the first lady of the college upon the hill, the wife of the president.

The role Betzi filled made no difference in her demeanor. She soon became known as "Mom Schroeder" to the students, even though she filled various professional positions on the campus. The responsibilities as Liaison to the President, Director of Conferences, and Adult Degree Completion Program Facilitator of Financial Aid filled her long days. When Nyack became the first accredited Christian liberal arts college in New York City, Betzi became the Administrative Assistant to the Dean. Nyack collaborated with many of the other ninety fine Christian institutions in the city to help make accredited degrees available to more students.

A TOTAL DEPENDENCY ON GOD

It was during this period of time that Betzi and I met. We both attended a function one night and sat at the same table. I was working to bring about the first prayer summit. Our table had a wonderful session of conversation, and I did not forget her.

When we began planning for a second prayer summit, Dixie Galloway's ministry responsibilities (see Chapter Five) did not allow her to continue. Consequently, we had a huge vacuum to fill. As I prayed, I immediately thought of Betzi, and the committee agreed. She eagerly became part of our Executive Committee because of her personal experience at the first prayer summit.

Betzi said, "I was profoundly overjoyed with what happened during the worship time. The church of God goes so far beyond just one denomination, and women coming together before the throne of God and worshiping was so powerful. I encountered God specifically in the first prayer summit. I was really drawn to Jesus. The presence of God was very evident during the whole time, and I had a lot of freedom to be able to say yes when asked to join the committee."

Betzi played a vital role on our Executive Committee. She planned and hosted one of our mini-prayer summits at the university. She worked tirelessly in selling tickets, planning, and participating in the second Women's Prayer Summit.

Years later, as she looked back upon her experience on the Executive Committee, she said, "I enjoyed working together in a peer relationship with mature Christian women. I was so blessed by the way the women honored and respected one another.

"The process was really fascinating to me. At all the mini-prayer summits before the second prayer summit, we focused upon 'The Armor of God.' I especially remember the visual impact of the six-foot-tall armored soldier (made of tin) that stood beside us at all six mini-prayer summits. Each of the committee members chose a piece of armor from Ephesians 6 to speak about. We put on the 'armor of God' to prepare for the big prayer summit, and that was significant.

"Every time we met, the goal was to step forward a little bit more to what the final program, the second Women's Prayer Summit, would look like. I was surprised by the need for structure for the program. Every minute had to be accounted for, yet the audience was so unaware of this.

"There was total and profound inquiry to God of what He wanted. There was no flippancy of self, but total dependency upon God. An idea would be brought forward, held before God, and then released to Him, seeking Him to give creativity for the Holy Spirit to draw women into His presence. We didn't want it to be man-made but God-led!"

BETZI'S MINISTRIES AFTER THE WOMEN'S PRAYER SUMMITS

"For me personally, the mini-prayer summits' concept of 'putting on the armor of God' proved significant because I was working with college-age students at that time. They are a generation of extremes. They are very committed and focused on wanting to know God's direction in their lives. They are radical, and they will step out in faith way beyond some of us who find that we hinder ourselves.

"My favorite role at the university was spiritual formation, where I walked alongside the students. I have found that I am a pastor at heart. As a result, I felt led to begin a Masters Program, which I completed in 2005. My calling is to facilitate emotional release given by God as we expose the lies that we believe about ourselves—to facilitate a personal healthy emotion. It is so exciting to find the heart of God in students, to be their spiritual cover, and to watch as God empowers them and leads them onward.

"They are also a hurting generation. They come with so much pain, whether they are suburban or urban kids. They come from all different lifestyles, and few are free from hurts. An extremely important question to ask them is what Jesus asked the man at the Bethsaida Pool, *Do you want to get well?* The way I interpret that whole story from John 5 is that they have to own their past as well as what they want to do with it. They must identify the lie that they believe about themselves and bring that before God, their Heavenly Father, and ask the Holy Spirit of God to breathe His truth into their lives. I am not necessarily asking for details, but I am asking the young person, 'What is the core that you believe about yourself?'

"There are so many lies that we believe because of our experiences. People have spoken negative things into our lives, such as *I don't measure up* or *God doesn't love me,* or *because of my promiscuity* or *because I have been sexually abused, I am not worth anything.* It's all those kinds of things that must be exposed.

"It is really amazing that as we release these perceptions to God—as we talk to God in prayer, asking for the Holy Spirit's presence and asking God to speak truth into our life, He does! I don't care how long it takes, but God does speak truth, and we ask for scriptural truth. We don't just want any psychological babble. The more we release to God in truth, the more our words in a spirit of worship can occur.

"Many of the students whom I have encountered did not have a good relationship with their fathers, and that pain begins to crack when they realize who God their Heavenly Father is. There is a great release in knowing they are loved by God. When this happens, I have seen lives turned around, and students become empowered. They are standing up on the inside, which is a very positive thing. They are empowered to go forward with God, and they are fearless.

"The more God fills us, and the more we place our lives in His presence, the more self-esteem we have, because we have the light of how God views us, how God sees us. We are His daughters, and He is a very loving Father.

"I had a visual for the students. In handing them a diploma, we actually handed them a baton because they are running the race, looking to Jesus, and He will go with them wherever they go. We were there behind them proudly cheering them on."

PRAYER MINISTRIES CONTINUE

Betzi continued, "My experiences in the first prayer summit as a guest and at the second as a committee member have had significance in my subsequent ministries. In the second summit, we had the huge cross on the stage, and we wrote down things of the past and symbolically nailed them to the cross. We left them there with Jesus that night. That was graphic and powerful!

"In the first prayer summit, the sense of unity in worship was very impacting. Because of that, I later became involved in another prayer movement, The Call NYC. Both were built upon the truth that the Body of Christ goes beyond one denomination, and that we are to be united and reconciled to one another. By that, as shown in John 17, we will show the world the unity between Jesus and God and that Jesus is love.

"At The Call NYC, eighty-five thousand believers gathered for twelve hours of prayer, worship, and fasting on June 29, 2002, at the site of the 1939–40 and 1964–65 World's Fairs in Flushing Meadows Corona Park.

"The logistical challenges of an event of this magnitude were further complicated by the fact that the tragedy of the Twin Towers attack on September 11 occurred just as we were beginning our dialogue with New York City pastors and leaders to plan about this historical gathering. Yet God, in His awesome faithfulness, defied the history of all other Call gatherings by enabling us to accomplish twice the work (two gatherings—one on June 22 and the Solemn Assembly on June 29—plus a week of ministry by youth on New York City streets) in half the time, January to June, with no greater budget than originally planned.

"Before The Call at Flushing Meadows, Nyack also had something called The Gathering. It sprang from a student's vision that we were to gather together in a local field for a day of fasting and prayer, for a day of reconciliation, for a day of repentance. There were different segments throughout the day with Lou Engle and those themes. About five hundred attended.

"One of the things we did was to have everyone gather and form one huge circle all around the field as we sang "When I Survey the Wondrous Cross." As we were singing and holding hands, a big cross was carried to the middle of the field to be set up. As this was happening, some people left the circle and just impulsively ran while others walked to the cross expectantly, for whatever our Lord Jesus Christ had wanted them to go there for. It was a humbling experience to see people at the cross.

"The day was just incredible. We had sunshine, wind, and snow—talk about the presence of God through the elements of nature. At that time there were reconciliations that needed to occur. A division existed between the college and the seminary, and we truly saw the Spirit of God working, making changes. A university model resulted, where they work together in convergence."

GETTING RID OF HIDDEN RESENTMENT AND ANGER

"While at Nyack during spiritual formation, I led others into prayer, asking God to reveal hindrances in their lives and seeking healing in those areas. However, God let me know there was an issue in my life, and He wanted it resolved! Chelsia was still in the Pennsylvania area with foster parents, but there had been no contact between our family and her, and that was the way I wanted it.

"Every time her name was mentioned, my husband and I experienced major discord. I would become childish, and he would become parent-like. Because I had always willingly moved, worked, and made any adjustment for ministry that was necessary, the family, and especially David, didn't fully under-stand how I felt, and I didn't explain it. My resentment and anger, kept under wrap and cover, nevertheless festered.

"The truth was that I was gripped by fear and stubbornness. I perceived that David had always chosen Chelsia's well-being over mine—and that hurt! I was expecting David to take her side in any future situation, and I would be rejected.

"One day in chapel, God confronted me with my fear about resolving this. He let me know that I was the one who had to take the initiative if this was ever going to be resolved. This was now a sin problem between God and me!

"I knew that I had to walk out in faith, rely on Him, step over the cliff, and let Him catch me. For ten years I had carried a phone number where Chelsia could be reached. I finally dialed the number and set aside a time for us to go meet with her.

"What I had expected for ten years never came to pass. David and I were totally united as we talked with her. He saw what I had felt. He apologized for forcing the issue upon both my son and me by using guilt as an enforcer.

"In fact, after we met with Chelsia, we made arrangements for her to enter Nyack her freshman year and live with us again. This was a wonderful time of unity for her and for our whole family. However, the academic life was too difficult for her, and she left after one semester. She returned to Pennsylvania, and we lost contact with her. Sadly, the last time we heard anything about her, she was on the streets. We pray she will return to Jesus, whom she professed as her Lord.

"My reason for sharing this is to advise the necessity for complete unity before couples or families make major decisions. Don't just acquiesce! For ten years I allowed disunity to exist in my family—rawness existed—but it didn't have to be that way. God wanted to redeem it long before I actually listened to and obeyed Him."

GOD WASTES NOTHING

Apprenticeship completion requires a logical sequence of duties and performances. Life experiences for David and Betzi proved to be an apprenticeship for a new experience.

They both felt complete freedom to accept a new assignment in July 2005. For several years David had served on the board of a global missionary ministry, International Teams. Because International Teams was going through a difficult time, the board of directors invited David to serve as president in the home office in Elgin, Illinois. Recently, however, he received and accepted a call to return to Christian higher education as president of Somerset Christian College in New Jersey. The new assignment seems to combine every aspect of any and all of their previous training and experiences.

Today's technology allows freedoms unimaginable only a few decades ago. From a New Jersey base, Betzi, with the heart of a pastor and her Masters Degree in Pastoral Counseling, will continue in her role as Missionary Advisor at International Teams to those in Central and Eastern Asia and Africa, as well as to interns, those who serve one day short of a year, and short-termers, those who serve less than three months. Her confidence is in her relationship of unity with her Lord. He will guide her in all wisdom, power, and strength.

From her relationship of service and unity with Jesus, a message burns within her heart: "One message that I would give to the women of tomorrow and the women of our nation is: release your children—release the next generation! This truth came to me a few years ago. We spent seven weeks with our missionary daughter and her family in Argentina. Her children were the only grandchildren we had at that time. As I was leaving the airport, amidst my tears, I realized that there was a release and a blessing that came from me to her.

"She was now establishing her own family traditions, establishing her own family unit separate from us, to live out the ministry that God had called them to, to do His will, and I was not supposed to be a hindrance but a blessing. Although we cannot physically touch them, with modern technology we have so much! We have the phone, the Internet, chat rooms, and digital cameras. Yes, it is painful, but we must bless and empower our children.

"When we empower and release them, our children want to come back. They are not living with guilt."

As you can see, God has answered the youthful desire in that little girl born to German immigrants. He has allowed her to represent Him all over the world to people of all walks of life—to people of all races, nations, tongues, and tribes.

WHERE AND TO WHOM CAN BETZI MINISTER IN THE NEXT TEN YEARS?
Anywhere and to anyone to whom God desires to minister through her.

WHERE AND TO WHOM CAN YOU MINISTER IN THE NEXT TEN YEARS?
Anywhere and to anyone to whom God desires to minister through you!

CHAPTER NINE

An Open Door—
An Open Hand—
Harlem for God

(WENDIE TROTT)

"EXCUSE ME, MAY I ASK A QUESTION?

DO YOU MEAN TO TELL US GOD

TOLD THIS WOMAN TO MEET

TOGETHER TO PRAY, AND WE'RE GOING

TO WAIT UNTIL 1998 TO DO IT?"

I heard the question and instantaneously knew that this was a woman from God for our Executive Committee. It happened during our last focus group in October 1996, in a room packed with women at a magnificent church on upper Fifth Avenue in New York City. This woman understood what God wanted to do!

The topic of discussion had been the timing of the prayer summit—should it be 1997 or 1998? From the beginning, I felt 1997 was the year, but others had advised that planning an event of this scope would require a minimum of two years. Following the scriptural mandate, *there is wisdom in many counselors,* although we discussed the question of timing at each focus group, we had reached no consensus. After Rev. Wendie Trott's question and comment, the responses were unanimous, as if to say, "Of course, we should pray in 1997!" From that point on, the year was never questioned.

God had recently transitioned her ministry from children to women. For many years, Wendie taught elementary school and had been a principal. She possessed an unmistakable leadership quality and radiated an inner spiritual perception that practically shouted the evidence of her close communion and walk with *Jesus.* I discovered the proof in my first telephone conversation with her; in fact, it was our first personal conversation.

When I called to ask her to join the Executive Committee and to take the leadership role of our Prayer Committee, she responded, "Yes, I will." Her next statement left me flabbergasted with delight. "I don't even have to pray about this. Two months ago, the Lord told our Bible study group to fast and pray and get ready for a job He had for us." That's what they had been doing—fasting to prepare for the Lord's call.

LEADING THE WAY IN PRAYER

The numerous circumstances that Christ orchestrates to bring answers to our prayers never cease to thrill me. How did Wendie Trott happen to be in that room that day? What prompted her to speak up?

She said, "Our head pastor received a phone call inviting a woman from our church to a meeting. I had begun working at the church earlier that year, was a brand-new minister in terms of my ordination, and was the woman on the Ministry Board. He asked me to go see what they wanted.

"I simply went to listen and tell him what was going on. But something happened in the meeting. The potential of the idea, of getting beyond the walls of my own personal ministry and being able to affect many more women in one place at one time, began to blaze within me.

"Women from other churches had already joined the women of our church in a new Bible study ministry. My goal was to help them to find their place in the Body of Christ. We met in various homes, and through this limited network, we had received many engagements to sing or speak. So the possibility of getting three or four thousand women together to sing and worship God and to let Jesus be the headliner intrigued me. The thought of being a member of the board and committee never entered my mind. I just wanted to be a part of something that would allow women from all over the city to come into one place.

"Even though I was blessed at birth with a Christian environment and grew up surrounded with a godly mother, father, and other supporters, I never viewed any of the women as my mentor. As I became an adult, I recognized the need in the Body of Christ for women to feel connected to one another and for female role models. Today's first-generation Christians don't even have mothers or grandmothers of faith to look back upon. So this seemed like a good opportunity for other women.

"However, it would become an unexpected ministry to me during one of the deepest voids in my life. Almost immediately after I had so quickly said yes, my mother became gravely ill. In spite of her twenty-year battle with the debilitating disease of multiple sclerosis and frequent hospitalizations, she had been relatively healthy. Although we had always known that some day it would take her, we didn't know when or how. I thought I was prepared for my mother to go, but when she was gone, I didn't think I could live. I had never breathed when she was not breathing, and the concept was totally foreign.

"The first scheduled Executive Committee meeting went on without me. I was at the funeral burying my mother. At the moment I didn't understand it. But, as the days, weeks, and months began to unfold, and we became busy in the Master's vineyard, in a whole new area and on a different level from anything I had ever done, it gave me an outlet for some of my pain.

"I realized that God had set me up—literally set me up—and had this fiery lady call to say, 'We want you on the committee.' *I thought, me? Why would she want me?* I had looked around that room, and there seemed to be a whole lot of women who seemed more educated, more sophisticated; they seemed to have a whole lot 'more stuff'!

"However, a week or two weeks later, I found myself in the room with women I barely knew, with a new challenge and a new focus."

Rev. Wendie took over the prayer network responsibility that the original prayer and fasting team from six states had so graciously provided for a little over sixteen months. The women of her Bible study committed to fast and pray for the Women's Prayer Summit for not only one year, but for two years! Was this a prophetic statement, or what?

In addition to her own Bible study group, she enlisted prayer networks from all over the metropolitan area—from churches, other Christian organizations, religious newspapers, and radio. She also led the devotional time at every committee meeting.

In addition, she, as did the other committee members, participated in each of our six mini-prayer summits (little commercials for the big event) and eleven women ministry leaders' meetings from February through May. That involved seventeen meetings over a period of eighteen Saturdays.

Her praying warriors were busier than ever from the beginning of June until October 4. This period of time was devoted to prayer and preparation for the Women's Prayer Summit in The Theater At Madison Square Garden. The last forty days before the prayer summit, August 25–October 3, she invited everyone she could contact in the metropolitan New York City prayer network to join her Bible study group and the Executive Committee in a rotational fasting and prayer time—as the original prayer group had conducted when God first implanted the seed back in 1995.

THE WOMEN'S PRAYER SUMMIT, OCTOBER 4, 1997

As Rev. Wendie stepped to the podium to open the first Women's Prayer Summit, no one suspected that a shattered heart beat beneath her chest. No one but God! He knew, and He displayed His approval in such a way that a friend upon viewing the tape of the prayer summit asked, "Who was the woman in the purple dress?" He said that he saw the glory of God literally surround her.

Wendie said, "He had no idea what strength his comment gave me. Even in our weakest moments, God sometimes just promises, *I will never leave you, but you are going to have to trust Me.*

"Through the prayer summit, I learned in a greater way how to be a balanced Christian. There are so many different varieties of the ways we serve God, and none of us is more spiritual or more favored by God than the other. We are just different. When you are center stage representing God, and God alone, there are things that you cannot do that, perhaps, you are at liberty to do when you are with your own peer group.

"The challenge of the day was to keep the focus upon Jesus. Though it didn't have to be any particular style, we knew that many of the women attending had never participated in different styles of worship other than their own. For them, this was a new experience. Therefore, each participant required a certain amount of spiritual maturity. The members of the board, every choir member, praise dancer—everyone who was going to stand before those women, whether it was to pray, teach, cry, apologize for the past—all those different elements that came together, everyone had to exhibit sensitivity. We had to find a way to be spiritually grown up enough to leave our personal ministering style to the side and find a way to engage doing a thing and not feel any less spiritual. That, to me, was an awesome thing. It was powerful, not just to be part of, but also to watch.

"I remember, in particular, a session targeting healing for victims of sexual abuse or abortion. We saw the impact it made! Women from all over the auditorium and even choir members audibly sobbed. Then and there we realized that God had entrusted us in that moment of time to literally bring about healing. The balm of Jesus was manifested in the lives of women we regularly see, smile at, and watch minister. But some of them had been serving Him with a limp. I watched the healing take place.

"For months after the event, women who ushered in those aisles, dressed in white blouses and black skirts, called, wrote, or came by to see me and told me what had happened to them. It had occurred as they just stood in the aisles, passed out the booklets and the offering baskets, and watched over the counting of all that offering money. They were amazed at God's anointing upon the women and the respect and reverential fear of God displayed in every aspect of the program. They said, 'There were all those women functioning together, and no one was fighting or arguing? No one was trying to push their way, but simply did what they were supposed to do and let God get the glory!'

"I will never forget the way God took care of every detail, even how the security people walked out of there with money in valises. Not a dime was lost, not one woman was pushed to the side, and no one came away from the experience feeling slighted. We demonstrated to the pastors of this city that we were not out to rob them of their members, but to help build the stamina of the women's ministries in their local churches. The effects are still being felt—ten years later.

"My daughters and the women in my ministry—all those

close to me—were there. I made sure they were exposed to the dynamics, and I watched the effect in their lives. Here were previously unrecognized women who, as a result of being part of the background, now have their own personal ministries in their churches. Some are missionaries, full-time pastor's wives, or have stepped into pastoral or teaching roles in their churches. The influence continues.

"The picture of watching that many women singing 'How Great Thou Art,' as some women lifted their hands and others didn't lift theirs, which mattered not to either group, gives us an inkling of what heaven will be like. Just a hint!

"Approximately two years before I met you, Janet, a prophecy had been spoken over my life that *God was taking me to the nations*. I didn't know what that meant, but as the curtain opened and I stood behind that podium and looked out over that array of women, I remember thinking, *Well, look at this. I went to the nations, and I didn't even have to get a passport.* I saw women with headdresses that indicated they were Muslims. There were Catholics and Protestants of all varieties. I remember thinking, *God has a way of allowing us to see, 'I birthed you for a purpose.'*

"As a result of being a part of that ministry and watching what God did in those women's lives at the church encounters, at the teas, as well as at the events themselves, I found myself going back to God and thanking Him for the awesomeness in which He created me. You look around and recognize that God was in every detail that surrounded even your birth and your destiny. He knew I was going to be called Wendie Gail. He even gave me a muscle that grew between my two front teeth that never allowed them to come together. He knew that I needed His mark upon me; that I would do what He said to do and go where He said to go. That was my experience."

LISTENING TO THE STILL SMALL VOICE

The first Executive Committee meeting after the prayer summit was bittersweet. Our euphoria faced reality. Among other things, we needed to discern whether or not God wanted us to have a second prayer summit. And I had to announce to Wendie and the rest of the committee that my husband and I would be moving in the near future.

As soon as God clearly revealed that we were to have a second prayer summit, we immediately went into action. The committee felt the need for a central office center in New York City, which is very expensive. Again, God provided. Bethel Gospel Assembly in Harlem gave us office space—rent free—next to Rev. Wendie's office. Diana Doleman agreed to be our administrative assistant. She was extremely efficient and handled everything with a delightful spirit. Everyone loved her.

As the months rushed by, the unknown was ever before us. Who was going to assume my role? There was no way I could ask anyone to take this volunteer responsibility. Only God could do that! And He did! He did it in the same remarkable way as He had provided in every other situation for the Women's Prayer

Summits. He had even placed her in the center of all the activity and decision-making for the second prayer summit. There was no doubt among the Executive Committee but that God had clearly appointed her to take on my role.

Near the conclusion of the second prayer summit, October 3, 1998, I passed the leadership of the Women's Prayer Summit and the Women's Prayer Summit, Inc. to Rev. Wendie Trott.

It was very difficult to leave these women whom I so dearly loved and with whom God had given a bond that today, ten years later, is as strong as ever. Yet I knew it was God's will. I knew that my work was completed, and the women were poised by God to move on—far beyond—without me.

What I didn't know was the reason God had chosen Rev. Wendie.

From the way God had opened hearts and doors for both of the Women's Prayer Summits and with all He had done through them, we all assumed that He planned for them to continue and to grow. Isn't that God's purpose—the expansion and building of His Kingdom?

Yes, He planned for the ministries of the women to continue and to expand. He also planned for His Kingdom to be strengthened and enlarged through these women, not only in the metropolitan New York City area but around the world. However, His plan called for a different blueprint.

One day in 1999, Rev. Wendie heard the *still small voice* of God (1 Kings 19:12) telling her, "Close the Women's Prayer Summit." Had she heard correctly? Why would He want to close this organization? It seemed the sky was the limit. Here she was, sitting in an exquisitely upholstered chair around a conference table in a downtown law office where people were saying, "We are going to work pro bono. What would you like?" She had increased the number of board members with new people whom she knew and trusted, and they were all comfortable with one another. She was, as were the other committee members, receiving speaking engagements from all over the area. She agonized over her message from the Lord regarding the future of the Women's Prayer Summit, Inc. She is human, and she struggled with the Lord. And He answered!

Wendie shared her struggle, "I was not above the temptation to take it somewhere, to force it to be something so that my name, perhaps, could become great. I said, 'Lord, I did not want to take this role, but you made it very clear I was to take it. Why did you ask me to take it, if all you want me to do is to shut it down?'

"He replied, 'I want you to close it with the same excellence with which it was opened.'

"God trusted me. He had given me something extra, and He knew that the tenacity He had put in my personality would not allow me to do something that He was not in the midst of.

"Janet, I still remember the last conversation we had. We returned to the church from a trip downtown. You were saying good-bye, and I wanted to cry, but I didn't. I remember your words, 'Wendie, don't ever be afraid to hear God. Now that you are taking the role of leadership, be careful not to push too many of your own thoughts. Let every woman at that table feel equal. Hear God and make the decisions you have to make, but let every woman know they are as viable in the organization as you are.' That helped me adjust my style of leadership as a woman, period!

"We were left with a viable organization and had two choices.

Go forward with excellence or don't go forward at all. To me there was not a third option.

"So within months I was sitting in front of the attorneys, telling them to draw up the papers and tell me the procedures. I watched the formation of a corporation and got a chance to sit in one of the most prestigious law firms in Manhattan and learn how to close down the corporation. I would never have known how to do that had I not gone to a meeting my pastor sent me to and simply said, 'Excuse me, may I ask a question?' That's all I thought I was doing! That's where you begin to understand how God designs and arranges things."

Rev. Wendie continued, "That day in the attorney's office was one of the roughest days in ministry I think I have ever had. I sat with women whom I highly respected. I had added a couple of men to the board because I wanted the pastors to know that though this was a women's event, we wanted to consult them. We did not have a problem with them at the table. These brothers said, 'Listen, if you think this is something that can be done, we have seen you do something out of nothing. But if God told you to close, we aren't going there.' The vote was over and done in two minutes.

"It was as much a lesson for us to close it that third year as it had been to open it. It was time for us to pray with the men. We had to come out from behind our little prayer closet where we said, 'You guys stay over there; we have something private to do.' We began to filter ourselves back into what the men are called by God to accomplish.

"That's how God led us to close the organization."

Challenged to Move to a New Level

Simultaneous with the closing of the Women's Prayer Summit, Inc., changes were occurring at Bethel Gospel Assembly, and Rev. Wendie experienced two more great personal losses. Health problems led the seventy-year-old senior pastor, Bishop Williams, who had faithfully served this great church for thirty-four years, to retire. Around that same time, Dr. Ruth Onukwue, who had become like a mother to Rev. Wendie and was her physician, announced that she was going to South Africa as a full-time missionary.

Wendie said, "Once again I had a lesson in learning how to let go. But with every level of letting go, God gave me a new challenge, a new level. When the bishop announced he was retiring, Pastor Brown said, 'I am not going to do this right now, but I want you to prepare yourself to take over the entire Women's Ministry of the church and take it city wide.'

"Okay," I said. "I looked as if I was fine, but as I walked out of the room, I felt my knees buckle. I heard the Lord's voice, 'Don't you realize the Women's Prayer Summit prepared you for this day?' The pattern looked familiar. I had not asked for a task, but God had trusted me with it.

"As I began to prepare myself, I realized something was wrong with me. I ended up in the hospital, and the surgery recuperation proposed to be seven weeks stretched into three long months!

"Just when I thought life was getting back to normal, I had to face my father's death. So I found myself, again in 2000, challenged with the grief over a lost parent. It was almost twice as devastating. I was so thankful that I had spent a lot of the past two years being with my father.

"Crisis followed crisis. Shortly after my father's death, I found myself in the hospital again, having more surgery. Edema overtook my body, and this time I was home for seven months.

"The two years following the prayer summit were tremendous lessons in survival. It all began after Pastor Brown handed me the ministry.

"The changed demographics of our area and church have also changed the needs of our women's ministry. We now have many women who have not been 'churched.' Many of them are dealing with life-controlling problems, sexual abuse, abortions, and all kinds of issues. My assignment was to bring in some young person. It wasn't me, because I was then forty.

"Using the model of the prayer summit board, I put together a board with many women whom I needed to get the job done.

"Of the many issues I learned from the Women's Prayer Summit, there is one main thing I loved and that I still talk about. When seven women were trying to discuss something and we could sort of feel a tugging, we would stop in the middle of a meeting and we would hear, 'Let's pray right now on this thing.' And still, we would stick to the agenda. We started on time, and we finished on time. Even though there were ten minutes for that, seven minutes for that, there was still time for us to stop and consult the Holy Ghost before we continued.

"I have six boards. They start and end on time. If there is a dispute, we stop in the middle so we can hear God. It is some-thing that I did not know how to do before the Women's Prayer Summit. I love the idea of lists and being organized, of not wasting our time or God's time, but being timely about what we do.

It's just like God gave me a little extra 'oomph' that I needed."

Back in 1997, Rev. Wendie had voiced a desire to develop a more systematic way to teach women how to rise above their circumstances and become who God had called them to be. In spite of her health difficulties and other challenges, which might have crushed most women, God expanded and moved the women's ministry forward. That dream became a reality as Alabaster Women of Faith emerged January 1, 2004. It incorporated graduated phases of individually-led education, encouragement, accountability, commitment, and worship to provide spiritual and social development and empowerment for women.

She was asked to become the Executive Director of Member Services. Every new believer or anyone receiving water baptism and/or membership in the church passes through Member Services and is assigned to a prayer group leader and a deacon. The church prays for the entire world. Each prayer group focuses upon a specific locality in the world. They study, go on mission trips, and pray for that area of the world.

"If You Sow Abroad, You Will Reap at Home"

Bethel Gospel Assembly celebrated its Ninety-Year Anniversary in November 2007. The goal of this extraordinary church is *Love, Learn, and Launch*! Perhaps it stems from their history. Ninety years ago, two young black girls confessed their sins and asked Jesus Christ to be their Savior at a downtown church in Manhattan. They asked to join the church but were denied membership. Lillian Kraeger, engaged to be married, volunteered to come to their home in Harlem and teach them the Bible. Her fiancé had a problem with that. He said, "If you do that—no wedding." She wisely did it, anyway! And there was no wedding!

That Bible study grew into a church built upon the *Rock* (*Jesus*) and has had only three senior pastors. Though Lillian never became a pastor of the group, she stayed with them until they grew large enough to form a church. She married later in life to someone more worthy of her.

Dr. Bishop Ezra Nehemiah Williams, the second pastor, served in that role thirty-four years. When he assumed that role, the Lord gave him a "word" that is believed to be key to the church's explosive growth: *If you sow abroad, you will reap at home.* He put it to the test in his first year of ministry with a mission trip to the West Indies. Some people left the church, complaining it could not afford such extravagance. History has proven how God felt about it.

He originally led them to buy a building located on 123rd Street and Lenox Avenue in Harlem. Bethel turned it into a house of worship and outgrew it. When a junior high school at 1832 Madison Avenue came up for auction, they were able to purchase it at a very reasonable price. The building held special significance for Bishop Williams because he attended school there. (He even recalls some less than pleasant experiences of chastisement there.)

When Bishop Williams retired in 1999, one of his two associates for twenty-five years, Rev. Carlton Brown, took his place. Bethel, a multi-cultural church (Asian, African-American, Caucasian-Hispanic, etc.), is broadcast over WMCA on Sunday mornings. They are picked up once a month by CBN.

In the last seven years, they have begun five new churches:

one in Virginia, one in New Jersey, two in the Bronx, and one in St. Vincent, West Indies. They organize five to eight short-term mission trips each year.

The former parking lot of the church has been excavated for the foundation of a new two thousand-seat auditorium, and on top of that will be a high-rise apartment building proposed to be fifteen to twenty stories.

Remember Dr. Onukwue, Rev. Wendie's physician who went to South Africa in 1999? A new elementary school and dormitory, Harmony Estates, has been funded by donations and largely built in South Africa by Bethel members on mission trips. Additionally, Dr. Onukwue returned with the funding for an orphanage for children suffering from AIDS and other issues, having raised the money during a month-long visit to New York City in January 2007.

If you ask Rev. Wendie whether her loss of a personal friend and physician has been aptly repaid by the knowledge of the existence of Harmony Estates and the fact that people in South Africa also have good medical help, what do you think she will say? If you have any doubt, these last paragraphs will wipe it away.

"I am blessed, not because of me, but because of my fore-mothers and my forefathers, who, I know, made a deal with God. Because God honored them, I've been a recipient of His blessing. That is my responsibility, to obey His voice, to not be flattered by flowery words, by money, by fame, by adulation. You do what God calls you to do, you do it the way He tells you to do it, and you trust Him to take care of the rest.

"And the picture of our committee members from the

Women's Prayer Summit goes in a special place on my conference room wall. It's a part of my history, and I plan to blow the picture up and put it in a frame in my home. I keep it here as a reminder. I like to keep every little part of my life that has been a stepping-stone close by to remind me of where God has brought me from and what He has entrusted me to do. I just remember to hold everything loosely. I don't hold on to anything tightly, because if you are not preparing people to take your place, you are not really ministering as 'unto the Lord.' "

WHAT CAN ONE WOMAN DO?

WHAT CAN REV. WENDIE TROTT DO?
Anything God wants to do through her.

WHAT CAN YOU DO?
Anything God wants to do through you!

CHAPTER TEN

The Father's Heart— For the Forgotten

(CAROL VEDRAL)

JESUS IS THE "CURE" FOR

SUBSTANCE ABUSE, POVERTY,

FAMILY STRIFE, WAYWARD CHILDREN,

AND EVERY EVIL AND CALAMITY

MANKIND CAN ENCOUNTER.

An unshakeable belief in this statement drives Carol Vedral to toil days, into the nights and weekends, so the often forgotten people of her city will know they are not forgotten, someone cares for them, and Jesus cares for them! To hundreds of people, she is the voice, the hands, and the human representation of Jesus. Her life is spent on their behalf.

Carol was the third woman to join our Executive Committee for the Women's Prayer Summit. The first time I met her I thought, *She looks like a china doll.* She had stunning dark hair and a porcelain face—features from her Italian heritage.

Both sets of grandparents emigrated from Italy and landed in New York City, where they raised their families. Carol is a third-generation believer. What a legacy!

Carol is best portrayed by a remark she shared during a casual conversation one day. She said, "The Lord revealed to me that I was not to fast from food, because He affirmed that my whole life was a 'fast' to Him." That was so apparent. After you have learned more about her, I have no doubt but that you will also agree.

We met at a focus group on Long Island. I learned that she had ministered beside her husband, Chuck, as he had served for many years as senior pastor at a church in Manhattan. It was the same church where, as a young man, he became a believer in Christ. At the time of our meeting, he had handed the role of senior pastor to his brother-in-law.

For decades the area of the city in which they ministered was a drug-driven community. Consequently, Carol and her husband served and ministered to many early cases of HIV infection.

In the late 1980s, during the height of the crack/HIV epidemic, when newborn babies were abandoned in hospitals by their mothers right after birth, the women of their church established a practical, hands-on ministry in Harlem Hospital. The babies and toddlers exhibited developmental delays simply because no one talked to them. Volunteers raised money for rocking chairs and socialized the infants through cuddling, rocking, singing, and talking to them—things that the overworked staff could not do. So that babies in the HIV/AIDS ward could hear language being spoken, they also raised money for a television set.

Carol did more! In response to the abandoned baby epidemic, she and her husband became foster parents in 1988. They cared for sixteen newborn babies over a period of three years. She became a vocal and persistent advocate for babies. Even though she perceived that some agency officials regarded her as a pest, she achieved her goal to bring some essential reforms to the foster care agency.

For ten years prior to our first meeting, Carol had organized women's spiritual retreats for their denominational conference. In addition to the fact that she was a spiritual powerhouse, this made her a natural to become a vital member of our Executive Committee to bring about a large women's prayer gathering.

With precious little time to develop strong and meaningful relationships, the Women's Prayer Summit Executive Committee had to communicate the vision and gather women from all over the New York City metropolitan area. I could hardly wait to get her on board.

God had prepared Carol in advance of our meeting. Our vision, proposed at the focus group, was in line with what God had clearly revealed to her that He wanted to do in New York City. She was ready to join with us, even though she and her husband had sensed that God was moving them toward a new ministry.

Carol was a gift from God to the Women's Prayer Summit. She networked and organized all of our six mini-prayer summit locations in 1997, as well as most of our leaders' meetings. She did this in spite of a health problem that adversely affected her voice. At times she was barely audible. In addition, she was an essential part of our Executive Committee meetings and the Women's Prayer Summit at The Theater At Madison Square Garden.

FATHER'S HEART MINISTRIES

As Carol and her husband listened to God's call, they responded. Carol tells how God spoke to them. "In October 1996, George Veach shared an amazing story regarding the outcome of Tommy Hicks' evangelistic crusades in Argentina in the 1950s. The harvest after three and a half years of ministry was more than five hundred thousand souls saved, but only one church of five hundred people emerged. *This was the result of not having laborers prepared to bring in the harvest.* He challenged Chuck and me to be ready to bring in the harvest that would most certainly come to New York City."

Their new ministry, of which Chuck would serve as president, would be headquartered in the same location as the church in which Chuck had served as pastor. It would enable them to reach out and assist even more people from their community. The Father's Heart Church members were in full agreement.

Carol said, "We started the Father's Heart Ministries, a faith-based 501(c)(3) nonprofit, in 1997 to prepare laborers for the harvest and to declare and demonstrate God's love and mercy. The vision and commitment of this ministry—to see the cycle of poverty broken and to see people go from dependency to dignity and from poverty to prosperity—could only be reached by addressing their immediate hunger needs, providing job preparedness and referrals, and offering prayer and spiritual assistance to help build a better future."

The demands of such a ministry are never-ending. Carol's responsibilities as Executive Director made it impossible for her to continue as a member of our Executive Committee to bring about the second prayer summit. However, she continued to serve as a board member of the Women's Prayer Summit, Inc.

"As the ministry was taking form," Carol said, "our mission statement became clear: Declare the message and demonstrate through ministry what is in God's heart. We told God's children that 'Daddy's not angry, and you can come home.' In the process of demonstrating the message of God's intention to love the world and not condemn it, we were to 'seek the lost, seek worshipers, and to prepare laborers to work with the population many believers shun, the forgotten people of the street and the poor.'"

You might inquire, "Who are the poor that God called Carol and Chuck to serve?"

"Some of the poor are homeless, but they comprise only about fifteen percent of the ministry. Many are ill, physically and/or mentally. Many have been sexually abused as children. When one is in a broken family and abused in this way, they generally have no one to go to or nowhere to turn. Because there is no one to help, they find ways to compensate, which is seldom good. Victimized people often seem to be targets and are perpetually victimized. A door has been opened by one event, and it is as if everything comes marching in behind it. People who have been victimized once seem to be victimized repeatedly and are often targets of demonic spirits.

"Others are lonely, despairing, beaten people, who may have lost all family members and who need and appreciate a welcoming, loving atmosphere more than food. There are many such people in the city. A huge immigrant population from China, Poland, Mexico, and other Spanish-speaking countries are in this category.

"The poor are also at-risk teenagers whose families have been disrupted by bad and even criminal decisions. The problems they labor under are often multiplied because brokenness has been ongoing for several generations. They face deficits of education, emotional support, and spiritual knowledge.

"Many live on fixed incomes, and some labor at low-paying jobs that do not provide enough income to meet their families' needs."

HOW THE WOMEN'S PRAYER SUMMIT AFFECTED THE MINISTRY

Carol says, "The experience of the Women's Prayer Summit created a greater hunger for the Word and prayer. I simply had to have more insight into God's Word. It also created a determination in my heart to find out specifically what God wanted me to do with my life. I realized that the many good things I was doing were not all 'God' things. I could only do *God-inspired work*, so other good things had to be released. In order to discern the difference, I had to develop a closer relationship with the Holy Spirit. It was the best decision I have made in my life, and I highly recommend intimacy with the Holy Spirit to all."

The *God-inspired work* took immediate form. Jesus said, *Feed my sheep* (John 21:17). There were hungry people in the neighborhood. So preparation began, and the word spread that all were welcome to be a guest for "Breakfast on Saturdays" at the Father's Heart Ministry in the old church building. Food, both physical and spiritual, waited for all the guests.

So they rolled out the welcome carpet at "Breakfast on Saturdays," and their guests are treated with respect. A seat at the table is waiting, and loving volunteers usher out a morning feast of eggs, sausages, potatoes, bread, fruit, coffee, juice, and milk. For some, this is the only protein serving of the week, and a bag filled with food is waiting for them to take home. If a guest requests more than one meal, another is served.

Carol tells of how an unusual but revealing situation occurred on a recent Saturday morning. "Herman (name changed) began to make a scene. For some reason, the guest sitting next to him upset him, and he began cursing the man. The volunteer quickly found another seat for Herman at a distant table and simultaneously placed a plate full of food before him. His head dropped almost to the plate, then he grabbed the fork and scooped the food into his mouth until the plate was empty. He asked for another serving, and another, and another.

"A different volunteer made his way over to Herman and asked, 'Hi! How is everything going?'

" 'Can you believe I have eaten ten plates of food?'

" 'I'm glad we could serve you, Herman. May I pray for you?'

" 'Sure!' "

"After the volunteer's prayer, Herman chimed in, 'Thank you, God. I really feel Your presence today.' "

"Without the breakfast program," said Carol, "Herman would never have agreed for someone to pray for him and would not have prayed himself. Obviously, he had not eaten for a while."

Carol adds another poignant story that demonstrates the amazing power of respect and love: "One morning in 1999, a man came in dressed in black from head to toe. A fedora almost covered his eyes, and a long trench coat hung on his body. He said to me, 'My name is Halloween.' Week after week he ate his breakfast, hunched over, never making eye contact with anyone. It was unnerving. Over the years, volunteers made countless efforts to befriend him. Slowly, his guard began to come down. He trusted us enough to reveal his real name, Peter (name changed), and other personal information. He eventually allowed us to pray for him. He changed his appearance, began to confide in us, allowed us to shake his hand, and finally permitted us to hug him. Peter, a graduate of Brown University, has schizophrenia; but with constant love and acceptance, he has gone from *scary* to *sunny*. Yes, *sunny*! He is no longer homeless. He allowed a friend from college to find housing for him. A gifted artist, he now spends his days creating wonderful sketches and watercolors."

In the early days of the Father's Heart Ministry, six hundred guests came for breakfast each Saturday. However, in the past

several years, other ministries have begun Saturday feeding programs in a park close by. Breakfasts are now more manageable
with four hundred guests, although the numbers are climbing
again. Thank God for the loving concern of others. Everyone
benefits when the labor is divided.

CREATIVITY + FLEXIBILITY + PRAYER = EFFECTIVE MINISTRY

To meet the needs of the poor, the Father's Heart ministry
exercised extraordinary creativity and flexibility. The method
they used was to first pray, and then think unconventionally.
Take courage and give away the beautiful oak pews. Then rip up
the carpeting in both the church and the small chapel behind it.
Replace the pews with folding tables and chairs so the environment is guest-friendly. However, much more than tables, chairs,
and food are required to make each Saturday meaningful!

Carol said, "The renewed emphasis on prayer that we
gained through the Women's Prayer Summit has played a most
significant part in our hunger prevention program. During the
course of the morning while breakfast is served and being eaten,
the ministry team moves throughout the room, offering individual
prayer and encouragement one person at a time. As is often the
case, once you pray for one, the guests nearby begin requesting
prayer. We have been thrilled with the many reports of answered
prayer over the years. *Prayer is the most precious and powerful
thing we offer our guests.* We are grateful for the assurance in
Isaiah 55 that God's Word does not return to Him until it
accomplishes the purpose for which it has been sent. Food is

consumed, and it's gone, but an impartation of the Word of God through prayer stands forever (Isaiah 40:8).

"Many of our guests are doing so well, we do not see them anymore. Through the years, some of our guests have returned with reports of a complete life change. They are no longer home-less, abusing drugs and alcohol, and are now working and serving the Lord.

"Tom, for example, is a joy to behold. He's one of the young men we repeatedly prayed for and encouraged. We ministered to him for years while he was high, angry, frustrated, yelling, or nod-ding asleep over his breakfast. Tom is a changed man today! He begged us to help him get into drug rehabilitation. We made sev-eral connections that failed. Finally, something clicked, and Tom was really ready. He followed through on the last contact. Two years later he returned to us with clear eyes, new clothes, gold jewelry, a car, a good job, and was living in an apartment. He came to thank us for not giving up on him. He was married last year, and this year, 2007, on their first wedding anniversary, they celebrated by moving into their new home. To God be the glory!"

Carol said, "Every Saturday morning our guests enter to the sound of worship led by Pastor Perry Hutchins. The worship is always lively and powerful. Guests come early, so they do not miss the music. They also respond favorably when prayers uttered with genuine concern for their well-being, translated by volunteers into Spanish, Cantonese, Mandarin, and occasionally Polish, ascend to heaven, appealing for Jesus' intervention in their lives. To close, we always ask for a response by the raising of hands, and those on the ministry team respond with prayer for each individual. Our guests are then invited to the platform for their social service needs: food stamps, housing, health care, etc. They are helped by professionals in the field, who volunteer their time.

SO MUCH MORE THAN FOOD

Over the course of 2006, a population shift of the Saturday guests was noticeable. More than half are Chinese, and 60 percent of the guests are 62 years of age or older.

Often seen out on the street collecting bottles is a dear old Chinese woman. She always wears black clothing, and it seems to accentuate her weathered and worn face. When she smiles, as she often does, her lips frame a toothless mouth. One Saturday morning she came in for breakfast and without pausing went to a back corner of the room, sat down, and bent over until her head almost touched her lap. The sound of her crying pierced the joyful atmosphere in the room as she became almost hysterical.

A volunteer rushed over and asked, "What is wrong?"

Through sobs and very little English, she finally communicated that her mentally ill daughter, who lived with her, was not taking her medicine and was out of control. The volunteer accompanied her home and convinced her daughter to take her medications. The next Saturday morning, this dear old woman gave her heart to Jesus.

Seeing Carol on the following Saturday, she flashed a big toothless smile and rushed over to her. With her strong fingers, she began massaging Carol's shoulders and said, "All is under control. Mom is happy now!"

Carol also recounts the story of another Chinese woman: "One Saturday morning, Angie (name changed), a slender Asian woman, came to the platform. The rapid movement of her head, the loud sound of her Chinese language mixed with a word or two of English, and her general body language clearly portrayed her distress. Pastor Marian leaned closer to Angie, but that didn't help her to understand the problem. Fortunately, a Chinese individual who spoke both languages came forward and translated. Angie was trying to tell Pastor Marian that her son, Jerry, had been incarcerated for a youthful offense and needed help. The young man remained in jail for ten years, much longer than his sentence, because his parents had immigrated to the United States and neither this country nor China wanted an ex-convict. Pastor Marian enlisted the aid of a Christian Chinese social worker, and through their joint efforts, the young man was freed. He was reunited with his parents in New York City. He stopped by during a Sunday morning service to express his gratitude. Jerry stood in front of the congregation and said, 'I have never been in a church in all my life, but I want to thank God and thank you for helping me.' Jerry quickly found a job, a wife, and just became a father. What an incredible way to be introduced to God's grace and love! This distraught mother came for food but found so much more.

"Often volunteers from all walks of life are referred to our feeding program and food pantry by the Food Bank for New York City and other secular agencies. One volunteer, Luis, came because he wanted to help people in a direct way. He became a regular, volunteering every week, and soon became a leader in the food service area. He was glad to receive the prayer we offered, and he also began to pray. He made a vow to the Lord that he would come to a Sunday service on his birthday. Luis kept his word. On his birthday he came to church and received Christ. He became a new man (Ephesians 4:20–24) and was immediately freed from years of heavy drinking and a bipolar disorder! Within a year and a half of his conversion, Luis married a Christian volunteer from one of the churches that support us, and now he and his wife are on the ministry team."

MINISTRY TO TEENS AND CHILDREN

"At-risk teens and children are not forgotten! Kidzone is our gang prevention/youth development program, and this area of ministry is huge! Every Tuesday night a fun meal is served to approximately one hundred and twenty or more children, youth, and family members. It might be food from McDonalds, pizza from Papa Johns, hotdogs, baked ziti, or even some other fun and interesting tasting concoction.

"During the evening, kids participate in an activity of choice. The options are many and appealing: creating arts and crafts, playing games, free guitar lessons, self-defense classes, and cooking nutritious snacks at the 'Fun with Food' nutrition table. Homework help is provided each Tuesday.

"Kidzone has surpassed all expectations and is becoming more and more like a community center. While the kids are participating in the program, family members often use this time to visit and socialize with other families within the community in a safe peaceful environment. They play chess, learn to crochet, or visit with friends. Both adults and children take home a 'goodie bag.' A prayer is always tucked into the bag. In addition, prayer is offered to all as they leave. Some kids will not leave without their 'blessing.'

"John," (name changed) says Carol, "is one of those kids. He often came alone just for the 'blessing.' The kids sometimes lead the parents. His mother now comes with him. She welcomes our prayers, and while her son is in Kidzone, she attends counseling sessions with our seminary-trained Christian counselor. John's father should be released from jail soon.

"Incidentally, our Christian counselor is one of our first converts. She received Christ in the late '70s. It is thrilling beyond words when God allows us to see the fruit of our labors.

"Kids join gangs for a lot of reasons. Some of them are the need for respect, support, recognition, identity, and money. Kidzone provides all these needs and more.

"Part of our gang-prevention program is Alphabet Scoop, our ice cream store. Not only do we sell delicious ice cream, but we make all of it ourselves. We determined that if we were going to have an ice cream business, the ice cream must be a good premium product. We wanted to establish a level of quality in the store.

"In 2003, we formed a committee of seven staff people. They thoroughly researched the ice cream business. We felt this could be a good opportunity to train our people, and that it could also generate income to help cover ministry expenses. The capital expenditure for the equipment was $25,000, which we did not have, but our God supplied!

"It was not an easy undertaking, but worthwhile things seldom are. We opened in March 2004, and even though our spring weather was terrible, it did all right. As time went on, we discovered the ice cream store did not meet all our goals. We felt the need to shift the business focus toward our teenagers and use this as a gang/prevention program. But we were uncertain as to how to make this change. God is so good and provided for us!

"One day a volunteer from a business consulting firm who packed groceries for us said, 'If you ever have a project that you need help in, contact us.' So we did. We took our ice cream business project to them. They gave us more than $50,000 of business advice. They came up with the clever name of *Alphabet Scoop*. (We are located in Alphabet City in the East Village.) They created a logo, chose our colors, and produced the awning outside the store.

"We had a grand reopening in April 2005. We recruit kids from Kidzone to work in the business, but we consider other applicants as well. More than twenty jumped at the chance to join our job training program to work in Alphabet Scoop. All applicants must agree to obtain working papers and participate in our mandatory training program. They are trained in practical skills such as making a variety of ice cream flavors, scooping ice cream properly, preparing shakes and sundaes, and using the cash register. They experience working under a mentor/manager and learn the importance of getting along with peers, of punctuality and appearance, and of managing their finances. These will be assets in all their future endeavors. More importantly, Alphabet Scoop is a safe work environment where youth can learn broader life and character building skills.

"We have twelve- and thirteen-year-olds begging to be included, even though they are too young to be hired. Undaunted, they volunteer their time because they want to be off the streets. To quote one ten-year-old, 'Will I live to be thirty?'

"Samuel (name changed), whose mother comes to the Father's Heart Church, just turned fourteen, a difficult age for most kids. His parents are divorced. No matter what his mother tried, Samuel did not want to come with her to church. However, he was recruited through Kidzone for Alphabet Scoop and has turned out to be one of our best trainees. Even though he was still thirteen when he joined the training program, we have uncovered a different Samuel. Of all the trainees, he is probably the most ambitious. He plans to take over as general manager one day. He is also one of our hardest workers, diligent with all his responsibilities, and very willing to take on new tasks. Samuel works under a Christian manager who is also a mentor."

The Father's Heart Ministries and Alphabet Scoop are participants in the Mentoring Partnership of New York, which is the local chapter of a nationwide organization. Carol has attended training and is now training more mentors.

A HOLISTIC MINISTRY

"Parenting Skills and Anger Management classes are offered three times each year. Sessions meet once a week for eight weeks. The curriculum has been approved by the New York City Administration for Children Services. At the time of this writing, all but one of the attendees of the class have been mandated to attend by Family Court. Most have had children removed from their homes. Perfect attendance is required to obtain a completion certificate to present in Family Court. (At the present time, no compensation is given to the Father's Heart Ministries for these attendees.)

"Continuous ESL (English as a second language) classes meet on Tuesday evenings and on Saturday mornings. All classes are free. A volunteer from NYCares taught these classes for a period of time but has moved on, and another volunteer from our church, a former NYCare volunteer, is taking his place.

"Our first ESL class was unique and astonishing. The students spoke Chinese, Polish, Spanish, and very little English, while the teacher spoke only English. The only way they could communicate was to use English, so they did quite well. Because they were the first group, they spent a great deal of time together, became very close, and occasionally had parties. Each nationality brought food from their native land. They learned enough English to be able to study for the test, and a few of them became citizens. Many of them found better jobs.

"But the defining moment of the class was the class just before Easter. The instructor asked the class, 'How do you celebrate Easter in your country?' Each told of their different customs, and then someone asked her, 'How do you celebrate Easter?' She told the story of the death of Christ and the resurrection. When finished, she gave an opportunity to receive Christ. All fifteen of them received Christ right there in the class.

"It was a very special moment. The teacher said, 'The presence of the Holy Spirit so filled the whole room that they all wanted Jesus! It was a powerful time.' "

Carol stated that every person is a story, some more heart-rending than others. "For years, Tina (name changed), a Chinese woman of approximately forty years, came and simply befriended me and all the staff. She spoke almost no English and wanted to attend the ESL class, but her husband would not permit it. Her eyes betrayed her loneliness, but her interest in everything revealed a keen intellect. She often just hung out at the church and talked with the staff. Her language skills began to improve somewhat. The staff would help her out all they could. They picked her up so she didn't have to walk everywhere. One day she said to Chuck, 'You are the only people who love me.' She went on to tell her story.

"She was a mail-order bride, sent by her parents in China to the United States because someone bought her. She was so lonely because she felt her husband did not love her. Her three children attended a good Chinese-speaking church in Chinatown. She would often say, 'My children in church, thank God. Thank God!' Now, two of them are in college, and the third child is in high school. She will not leave the 'Breakfast on Saturdays' until a staff member prays for her. She says, 'Thanks to God. Jesus helps me.' "

STAFFING WITH VOLUNTEERS AND FINDING THE FUNDS

Carol said, "We could never do this work without our twenty wonderful, faithful core volunteers and the over seven thousand who help us annually! They never get the credit they deserve. Everything I have done over the years has been in collaboration with others."

The Father's Heart Ministries has four full-time staff members who serve sacrificially. Chuck and Carol and Perry and Marian

Hutchins (Carol's sister and brother-in-law) all presently function as pastors in the church and the ministries. Marian oversees the food pantry and soup kitchen operations, Kidzone (also with a soup kitchen), ESL and Parenting and Anger Management classes. Chuck doubles as the accountant, and he and Marian handle all the food grants. They all do double and triple duty—whatever it takes.

To fund such a large ministry, Carol said, "You hear a lot of talk about living by faith, and we have been doing it. God has been faithful to supply our needs. There are pretty scary times, but God always comes through. It is only God. I have no formulas other than to say that we just cry out to God. We say, 'Help us, God. Help us, please.'"

This has to be the most difficult part of her job. She sees the needs of the people, but every program requires resources, and when they are not available, the programs cannot continue. They network with other agencies to provide food stamps, health care, housing advocacy, computer classes, and other services.

All their grants for food come through city, state, and federal agencies, but they receive no cash. They receive an account at the Food Bank of New York City or other agencies and are able to order food. Other agencies they work with are: NYC Coalition Against Hunger, Community Food Resource Center, City Harvest, America's Second Harvest, United Way, the Chinese-American Planning Council, Department of Youth & Community Development, NYCares, Emergency Food and Shelter NYC Board Program, the Emergency Food Assistance Program (EFAP), NYC Workforce Investment Board (WIB)

Housing Bureau PSA 4, the New York Junior League, and the NY Legal Assistance Group.

However, it is never enough. Remember the gentleman who ate ten breakfasts? Well, they are reimbursed for only one breakfast per person, and many people request more than one plate full of food—and their guests are always offered more food. The Father's Heart Ministries pays for their plates, napkins, etc., and are occasionally partially reimbursed.

Other churches, corporations, organizations, and individuals from the New York Junior League are donors. Con Edison has sponsored the Kidzone Christmas party for the past three years. They provide lots of food and dozens of gifts. A real estate firm has been particularly generous the past few years and occasionally treated the Kidzone program to meals of chickens, rice, and beans. Everything else comes through private donations.

The grants have been increasing year by year, and they need them. In November 2005, the food pantry had to be closed because there were not enough volunteers during the week. Most people are working when food deliveries arrive on Tuesdays and Wednesdays. Again, God worked! America's Second Harvest provided a grant for stipends for workers to bring in and store food deliveries and bag groceries for distribution—enormous tasks. Over eight hundred people are registered in the food pantry.

Carol says, "The provision of income for food pantry workers has created other benefits, the greatest of which is the transformation of lives. For thirty years we have served a substance-abusing community through the spiritual activities of the

Father's Heart Church. We have longed for a work program for those we are helping. We know that they need money to sustain themselves, but they also need loving support, guidance, and training. The stipends are enabling us to have a work program of sorts. We recruit these men from our 'Breakfasts on Saturdays.' They work under the direction of Rev. Perry Hutchins, who also oversees the Food Pantry Coordinator. Pastor Hutchins ministers weekly in Beth Israel's substance abuse rehabilitation center. He also directs a weekly twelve-step meeting in our church."

THE AMAZING VALUE OF A WORK PROGRAM

The following report from Carol shouts the value of their work program (names withheld):

"After working in the food pantry, one person got a full-time job in a work program in Philadelphia.

"Two men stopped drinking.

"Another requested that we save his weekly stipend for him until he had enough money to pay a month's rent for an SRO. He was able to get out of the shelter and is now living on his own and still works with us. He has been reconciled with his mother and has regained the respect of his family.

"Another had lost his job as a porter and was depressed and downcast. He came to volunteer to pass some time. By receiving a stipend, small as it is, it seems to have restored his dignity to some degree. He is happy to be mentored by a pastor and to also have a confidante.

"Another is learning to manage his money. For the first time he has been able to save his money and buy things he wants, such as a cell phone. This makes communication much easier. He has been getting job offers and is climbing his way out of poverty.

"Another has become a reliable worker. He also comes to volunteer at our Saturday breakfasts.

"Another got his own apartment and, as a result, was reconciled with his daughter.

"Another, after working with us, got a job with the city of New York as a custodian at a public school.

"Still another worked with us a short time before he got a full-time job installing cabinets.

"On the whole, the guys have learned to be on time, to work hard, get along with one another, and to take pride in a completed project. Much mentoring goes on during work. We also provide them with coffee, juice, snacks, and lunch during work hours. The whole atmosphere creates a feeling that there is a foundation of people behind them, encouraging them, helping them, and pulling for them.

"But there is always more to be done. There are medical, dental, and mental health clinics, transitional centers, and charter schools to be launched, more meaningful programs and outreaches for teens, for pregnant teenagers, for battered women, for the elderly, for the despairing and suicidal.

"All of these are inspired by a loving Father who has heard their cries. It is 'through His church'—through the ones called out of darkness, cleansed by His blood, who resemble His Firstborn—it is through His own children, His family on earth, you and me, that He chooses to reveal His wisdom.

"God wants to 'strut His stuff' to invisible and visible

witnesses, and we are thrilled and humbled that He is doing it through us on East 11th Street in Manhattan, New York City. This was His intention all along, and we were blessed to stumble upon His plan."

LET GOD REVEAL HIS WISDOM AND PLAN

God's plan for the Father's Heart Church members was to share with the community—with those who, most likely, would not worship with them on Sunday. They gave up their traditional pews for the sake of others. As it turned out, they decided the format used for "Breakfasts on Saturday" was so good that they similarly changed their format on Sunday mornings.

Their first hour is called "Breakfast with the Pastors." They sit around the tables to enjoy bagels, bialys, doughnuts, coffee, and juice. The pastors move around to chat one-on-one and to pray with the congregation. The second hour everyone joins in worship (music and prayer), the preaching of the Word, and any other customary elements, such as communion, water baptism, baby dedication, etc.

God's plan also called for the Father's Heart Network of Ministers and Churches to develop and provide training for new laborers. The legacy of faith from the four Italian immigrant grandparents lives on to the fourth generation in these new laborers. Two of Carol and Chuck's children and a son-in-law actively assist in the ministries.

God's plan was for Carol to serve Him as Executive Director of the Father's Heart Ministries. This is the woman whose whole life is a "fast" to her Lord, Jesus Christ.

As Carol and I were bringing our interview to a close, I asked this mother of six and grandmother of five if she had a word to give to you, her sisters.

She replied, "Do not be deterred in your pursuit of God and His will for your life. Do not let gender, age, lack of training or education, disappointments, failures—ANYTHING—keep you from the high calling of God in your life. Let the Holy Spirit be your best friend. He will open the eyes of your understanding. He is the Spirit of wisdom and revelation. He will let you know how to deal with all the negative things that are coming your way. The opposition you face is from a defeated foe—don't let him trick you.

"Remember this glorious promise from Ephesians 3:10–11: *His intent was that now, through the church, the manifold wisdom of God should be made known to the rulers and authorities in the heavenly realms, according to his eternal purpose which he accomplished in Christ Jesus our Lord.*

"Let God reveal His wisdom—for sin, sickness, bondage, poverty, and loss—through you."

AGAIN, I ASK, WHAT CAN ONE WOMAN DO?

WHAT CAN CAROL VEDRAL DO?
Anything God wants to do through her.

WHAT CAN YOU DO?
Anything God wants to do through you.

CHAPTER ELEVEN

LORD, What Can I Do?

(MARLI SPIEKER)

"LORD, WHATEVER I CAN,

I WILL DO TO BRING HER

TO THE LIGHT!"

Marli rushed into the air-conditioned mall to use the public phone located close to an automatic door. The palm of her hand instinctively swept across her hot cheekbone and up to her hairline to brush wet hair away from her forehead. A glance at the outside thermometer left no doubt as to why she felt so miserable and why her clothes were nearly dripping water. It was 104°F! That temperature coupled with a humidity reading in the 90s was not uncommon in this otherwise beautiful city of Singapore.

Her telephone conversation ended abruptly when she caught sight of a young couple approaching the same door through which she had entered the mall. Something caused a cold chill to come over Marli . . . it was the way they were dressed.

Marli said, "I looked at the woman, then the man. He was young, so I assumed she was also young. I felt a seething sensation rise up within me. She was dressed in hot, heavy black material from head to toe, with only a little net over her eyes. Her husband, though, was wearing a cool little cotton T-shirt. I hung up the phone and walked farther inside the mall and slumped down in a chair near a table. 'Lord, that is so unfair,' I said.

"As I sat there, I felt as if the Lord said, 'Do you see that black veil? It is not only over her head. It is over her mind, her heart, her family, her spirit, her whole life! This woman lives in darkness.'

"I responded, 'Lord, what can I do?'

" 'What do you hold in your hand?'

"Radio had been my ministry in Brazil, but that was before we had moved to the United States. I had hosted a children's program for more than thirteen years, a woman's program and other adult programs for five, and I knew the Lord was referring to a microphone. 'Lord, whatever I can, I will do to bring her to the light!'

"As I spoke those words, my life flashed before my eyes. I thought of my parents. My mother. What a woman! With only two years of formal education, she had still become a knowledgeable woman and had for years written a newspaper column for the largest newspaper in our city. Her insatiable desire to study and learn new things continued until the day she died. She and my father, a tailor, met in Sorocaba, São Paulo, Brazil, and they married at very young ages. By the time my mother was eighteen, she had given birth to my three brothers.

"Life was very busy for them, and it was not easy, but they settled into a routine. They cared for their young family, worked long hours at the shop, and attended a local Presbyterian church. One particular day, however, their lives took a drastic turn. They discovered it was possible to have a personal relationship with God through faith in Jesus Christ! Along with their newfound faith came a revolutionary change in their lifestyle. They became avid students of the Bible, soon progressed to teaching classes on Sundays, and began going out on the street, with their babies, telling others of their discovery.

"When they became acquainted with the Salvation Army in Brazil, they immediately connected with the Army's strong outreach to the poor and un-churched, their joyful services with drums and exuberant worship, and the Cadet Bible School. After a year, they accepted an assignment to lead a church and to work among the poor in the city of Curitiba. Then they were asked to run an orphanage with forty boys.

"This was the family into which I was born—three biological brothers, ages six, eight, and nine, and the orphanage boys. As I grew, I especially adored my oldest brother, Celso. He was so good to all of us. He carried me everywhere, pampered me. I loved it and him!

FOLLOWING IN HER MOTHER'S FOOTSTEPS

"Five years later, my parents were transferred to a much worse orphanage in the extreme south of Brazil in the city of Pelotas, where, at that time, evangelicals were labeled as a *sect*. In this orphanage my parents found a group of around twenty malnourished, sick, and dirty kids. Some of them had deformed ears because the rats had bitten them as they slept. They had hardly anything to eat or to wear. I do not know how my parents managed or survived. They received no extra funding from the Salvation Army. The government sent kids but never paid for their expenses. My father regularly went out in a horse-drawn buggy with my two older brothers and literally begged the local people at the market or grocery stores to give something to the orphans. They often returned with little.

"It was during this time that my life as a happy, loved, and protected little princess of five was turned upside down. My loving oldest brother, whom I adored, left home one morning and never returned! I never saw his smiling face again. I never again felt the security of his big arms carrying me around. At five years of age, I did not understand all the implications of the news pronounced to my mother and father. I only knew I missed my brother! We learned he had been riding his bicycle and had collided with a vehicle. It was the coldest, most forlorn, and devastating night our family ever experienced. My father stayed with my mother at the mortuary with my brother's body as long as he dared—no one was attending the orphans. My mother spent the rest of the night alone at the mortuary with no family and no friends to comfort her. She had only her God!

"Even though my parents endured untold grief, they never stopped caring for the orphans. Interestingly enough, the people of the city developed a different attitude toward my parents and their work at the orphanage after my brother's accident. They became more willing to contribute food and clothing.

"However, for me life took an even worse turn—one that proved to be the next most difficult of my younger years. After my brother's death, my mother was afraid she would also lose me. It almost became an obsession. The orphanage, with boys from four to eighteen years of age, was a dangerous place for a five-year-old girl. The vast majority were troubled kids with all kinds of emotional damage from abuse of every kind.

"A kind and generous woman, whose name I have never learned, paid my tuition to attend an elite boarding school for girls in the city of Pelotas in Rio Grande do Sul state in south Brazil. Although it was a safe place, and I obtained an education that only the wealthiest of families could afford, learned good manners, and acquired a love of music, art, and beauty, it was a painful place for me to be. Night after night, my tears soaked my pillow as I cried myself to sleep.

"When I lost my oldest brother, it was almost as though I also had lost my parents and my two other brothers. I was all alone. For the next six years of my life, there was no one to give me any positive reinforcement. If I did something wrong, I heard about that. When I was sick, no one *mothered* me. Other than my grades, I felt devoid of affirmation.

"There was another element of boarding school that was hurtful, and its memory lingers to this day. The other students made fun of my simple handsewn clothes. They received all kinds of *care packages.* I received none. Their parents were able to visit them often, but mine were never able to come. Rather than feeling privileged, I ended up feeling abandoned.

"My perception of abandonment turned into a deep sadness. It was a sadness that almost suffocated me. Sometimes I felt as if I could not inhale enough air to breathe another breath. This sadness turned into resentment against the God of my parents for taking them away from me for so long. After I returned home, I sometimes resented my mother's care and concern for all *those people who needed help.* After all, I had needed her for six years, and instead of caring for me, she had been caring for the orphans, other sick and homeless people, and for prostitutes.

"It was not until I was fifteen years of age and found I could have a personal relationship with Jesus that my whole attitude was changed. At sixteen, I entered the Salvation Army Bible School, even though I was noticeably under the entrance age requirement. I began following in the steps of my mother, working in the slums, the brothels, the bars of big cities such as São Paulo and Rio de Janeiro, and giving hope to the hopeless. That included feeding them, providing places for them to bathe, and then telling them about Jesus and His love for them.

"My flashback flushed up many unhappy memories. I remembered the sorrow I experienced from rejection and betrayal of two close friends I trusted. I recalled the devastation I felt and the pain of losing my father in a terrible car accident when I was twenty. It happened as he was driving to a Salvation Army open air meeting in downtown Curitiba to preach.

"My only human comfort was Edmund, the handsome, well-respected, brilliant, but penniless German seminary student. We married on February 12, 1966. I was twenty-one, and he was twenty-six. The happiness and joy we experienced began to push those unhappy boarding school memories far down into my sub-consciousness. In fact, I would never again, to this day, feel unloved, unappreciated, or devalued."

LEARN A NEW LANGUAGE AT THE AGE OF FORTY?

Marli and Edmund Spieker joined Trans World Radio (TWR) Brazil on May 15, 1969, with the task to establish TWR's ministry in Brazil. They produced radio programs in Portuguese and took care of all the follow-up work. Marli had just turned twenty-four. Her education and experience in learning how to handle hard things began to pay off as God began to bless their efforts. Marli's gift and ability to speak and teach over the radio soon became apparent as the next fourteen years proved. Communication was her strength, language her ease of expression, and she enjoyed it!

Far from her mind was any thought of the approaching circumstances that would replace her strength in communication with great frustration, yet be the very thing to open the world to her. Though she was unaware of it, the tool Marli lacked in order to be prepared for her next big assignment from God was English.

Then came the offer from TWR: "We would like for you to temporarily move to Canada and then to our headquarters in Chatham, New Jersey."

The United States? After much prayer, Marli and Edmund felt a definite leading from God to leave their home, their home country, and everything familiar, including their language.

Marli did not come to the United States in strength but in weakness. She came with the handicap of being unable to easily and effectively communicate. But the Lord assures us, *My power is made perfect in weakness* (2 Corinthians 12:9).

"To learn a language at forty was the biggest challenge I had ever faced in my life," Marli said. "It was something that I knew would depend upon my own effort and perseverance. My tongue had been my instrument to serve God all my life, and now I could not speak right—at the age of forty! It was all very humbling and extremely challenging."

One might think a move to Chatham, New Jersey, approximately thirty miles from New York City, with a sixteen-year-old son, Marcio, a twelve-year-old daughter, Simone, a nine-year-old son, Fabio, and a language barrier would be a difficult adjustment for Marli. But that is not how she describes it.

"I had just arrived in *Alice's Wonderland!* I never dreamed of coming to this country, but I remember falling in love with it the first fall in Chatham, New Jersey. The beauty was intoxicating. I had never seen, even in western Canada, the spectacular fall foliage I saw two months after we arrived in New Jersey."

Marli went on to state, "The greatest challenge in this move was my duty as guardian of my treasure, my family. We had already lived in three different countries, and I knew that we needed to keep ourselves united, secure, and contented in God's arms. This move was His idea, not ours. The challenge was to keep the external influences and struggles away from the center of who we were, without hampering or preventing us from becoming who God wanted us to become.

"The church God led us to attend, Long Hill Chapel, also became my home and my family. I remember being alone in my house as big warm teardrops rolled down my cheeks, but they were not tears of sadness. They were tears of joy and gratitude as I experienced the goodness of the people God had placed in our lives. The loving warmth of my new family and home was over-whelming. They loved us, and especially loved our children. That was so comforting, so welcoming."

How does one minister when one does not speak the language?

"It was hard. I immediately began offering to help at our church. I had difficulty speaking, but I could use my hands. I cleaned and organized and offered to help with anything that needed to be done at the church. To my surprise, in spite of my broken English, they invited me to lead the Women's Missionary Prayer Fellowship and then to become a deaconess. I also helped with hospitality at TWR. I think this was all part of God's train-ing for me to do what I do today."

I first met Marli when she spoke in a women's meeting in our church. Although I had difficulty understanding everything she said, I knew this was a woman I wanted to get to know. We became fast friends.

I watched as she tackled the challenge of learning English, and as she and her family adjusted to a new culture. I watched as she faced the challenge of living on a missionary's salary in an affluent East Coast neighborhood. I watched as she traveled alone at night into a much less affluent area where many Brazilians lived. She helped them adjust to a new culture; she taught them biblical principles to help stabilize their families; she counseled them, and most importantly, she loved them. I watched as she fluidly moved from one socio-economic grouping of people to another, all the time feeling at ease in any social situation in which she found herself. I watched as she crossed one hurdle after another.

When TWR moved their headquarters to Cary, North Carolina, in 1990, and the Spiekers followed, Marli and I kept in close contact. They were able to purchase a lovely property, something they could never have done in the expensive New Jersey housing market. When they moved into a new church and knew no one, both Marli and Edmund volunteered to serve in the nursery. It was not long before Marli invited some of the young mothers to her house for a tea. The young women asked her to lead them in a Bible study, and the group began to grow.

"GOD HAS SOMETHING BEAUTIFUL FOR YOU THERE"

Back in New Jersey, approximately five hundred miles from North Carolina, when God gave me the vision for the Women's Prayer Summit in August 1995, Marli was one of the first people I called. She was one of the women in our initial forty-day rotational fasting and prayer team. The distance did not prevent her from traveling to the New York Area several times for meetings.

One day the telephone rang, and I heard the concern in her voice. "Marli, what is wrong?"

"Well, Edmund called last night from Singapore, and he asked me to join him there. He comes back home every three weeks in line with the mission travel policy, but the travel time and jet lag combination reduces his productivity. He feels he could be much more effective if he were able to have a more permanent base there. In addition, he is certain that God has something for me in Asia—details unknown, of course! But we have always been a team, and he needs me!"

"Well, Marli, you know what you need to do."

"Oh, I know, but I cannot bear the thought of leaving Stephan [her first and only grandchild] and missing all the cute things he does, of watching him grow. Then, there are Fabio and Simone and their new spouses. I very plainly do not want to miss the fun of seeing them establishing their homes. To say nothing of my young mothers, eighty-five of them now, and their eleven mentors and leaders. They are really my dearest friends. Do I walk away from a ministry that God has given me? Can I just leave?"

If you have ever moved as an adult woman, you know how difficult it is to leave your family, work or ministry, organizations and responsibilities, friends, home, neighborhood, favorite stores, familiar food markets, and bargain spots. You know how frustrating it is to have to find new doctors, dentists, to learn your way around a new city, to say nothing of learning the shortcuts to avoid traffic. Marli had left her home country of Brazil, moved to Canada and lived there for two years, moved to the metropolitan New York City area for six years, lived in North

Carolina for five years, and now was faced with another move to another country, just as she was feeling at home in North Carolina. No wonder the thought was unsettling!

However, by the time we finished talking, she had concluded, "Yes, it will be hard to miss out on Stephan's developmental changes. And, in all reality, Fabio and Simone will probably not need a mother as much anymore. And, yes, God can give another ministry with women." But the underlying principle to her change of heart was Edmund's certainty that God wanted her to come to Singapore.

Edmund's role of International Director at TWR did not include per diem expenses for Marli. If she were to accompany him, they would have to pay her expenses. Since few missionaries have bulging bank balances, they must be ingenious and flexible. Marli and Edmund sold the house they had so thoroughly enjoyed while living in North Carolina, put all their personal belongings in storage, and used the money normally budgeted for a house payment to cover Marli's expenses.

Edmund kept assuring Marli, "God has something beautiful for you there. I know He has!"

Their first trip after arrival in Singapore was to Guam, the location of TWR's powerful transmitters and studios. While Edmund was in meetings, Marli took the old mission car and drove to a deserted beach. She said, "I had my Bible with me. I was hoping God would talk to me and give me an answer to my suggestions as to what I might do. I needed to feel God's love in the move. I needed to know that His love was guiding and that He would protect us from our own ways. Basically, I needed to be certain we were in the center of His will."

God had a message for her that morning. She opened her Bible to Jeremiah 18:6: *Like clay in the hand of the potter, so are you in my hand.* Marli said, "I closed the Bible. God was talking to me, but I did not want to hear that kind of message. I opened the Bible again to my favorite prophet, Isaiah. My eyes fell upon verse eight of chapter sixty-four: *Yet, O LORD, you are our Father. We are the clay, you are the potter; we are all the work of your hand.* I closed the Bible quickly. I felt as if God were in that old car staring at me. I did not want to hear that message. So I tried again. Romans 8 has blessed me so many times, so I opened up to chapter eight and kept reading on into chapter nine when verse twenty jumped out at me. I could not believe it! *But who are you, O man, to talk back to God? Shall what is formed say to him who formed it, "Why did you make me like this?" Does not the potter have the right to make out of the same lump of clay some pottery for noble purposes and some for common use?*

"God brought me to my senses. I broke down and once again relinquished all my rights, my plans, and my will—my resentment about leaving my grandson, children, friends, house, and ministry—to Christ. I understood so clearly: 'Yes, I am the clay, Lord. Clay does not rebel, does not make plans; it does not even talk back. Clay abandons itself in the potter's hands!' "

And it was that abandonment that led the Potter to show the clay what He had in store for her. He revealed it to her that day in the mall in Singapore, after she watched the couple walk through the door. He wanted her back in radio. He wanted her to reach His suffering women all over the world. But something needed to be added to the radio programming, something much more powerful than even those super-powered transmitters—the *mega power* of a fasting and prayer ministry.

WITNESSING MEGA POWER

To those who watch God at work, nothing is more astounding than to look back upon the various avenues of preparation He provides for the job He wants done. English was a prerequisite for the job God had for Marli, and He had provided that. He illustrated the *mega power* of fasting and prayer during her involvement with the early prayer preparation, the forty-day rotational fasting schedule for the Women's Prayer Summit. She watched as He opened doors, brought people, and gave guidance.

The Spiekers made periodic trips between Singapore and the United States. On one of those trips in 1997, Marli spent a weekend in New Jersey. I had a surprise to show her—the unfolding of God's answers from previous prayers. We drove into New York City and sat on 7th Avenue and watched as the greeting, *Jesus Bids Us Come . . . to the Women's Prayer Summit . . .* flashed upon the famous Madison Square Garden marquee every twenty minutes. Ten years later she said of that moment, "A great blessing I received was the day you and I went to the city to see the invitation about the prayer summit on the Madison Square Garden marquee. I saw firsthand what one woman with a passion was able to do if she would trust and obey God's prompting to step out of her comfort zone. She could have the call of Jesus highlighted on a world-famous secular marquee! If God could so use one ordinary woman—not a missionary, a preacher, or a director of any Christian missionary organization—He could use anybody, even me."

Four months later, Marli returned to the United States to attend and participate in the first Women's Prayer Summit in The Theater At Madison Square Garden. She came with a broken heart. While in Asia, it seemed that every place she turned God had opened her eyes to the plight of suffering women and persecuted Christians all over the world. At the Women's Prayer Summit, she prayed specifically for believers who were being jailed and for those whose very lives were in danger because they followed *Jesus*. At that time, few American women were aware of the persecution many believers around the world were experiencing. The loss of educational opportunities, jobs, and homes, just because one believed in Jesus, were foreign to them. When Marli's prayer included situations such as bondage, trafficking of children and young women, the sale of children into prostitution, the sale of women for as little as fifteen dollars, poverty, abandonment, and homelessness, the prayer summit women did not just pray with her, they cried tears of empathy.

From the Women's Prayer Summit, Marli went back to Singapore and met with her prayer team of twelve Chinese women. With her husband's encouragement, she presented to the Asia Pacific Ministry team the first draft of a proposal for a radio program in magazine-style format that would feature testimonies, meditations, music, and practical and spiritual advice to help women cope with their daily plight.

The following month she returned to the United States and met with the president of TWR. She presented the concept of a new worldwide outreach to women that would not just be *Radio Broadcasts* but also *PRAYER* and *Awareness of the Plight of*

Suffering Women in the World, the three aspects of a vision that would become Project Hannah.

Marli said, "At that time, TWR's excellent worldwide ministry was broadcasting a few women's programs in some countries. However, there was not an intentional strategic 'women's ministry.' When I received the vision and understood the importance and extreme need for such an outreach ministry to suffering women worldwide, I felt like little David with Saul's armor (1 Samuel 17:38–39).

"There was an understanding that if the husband, the head of the household, could be won for Christ, the whole family would follow. However, statistics confirm that today the majority of worldwide households are run by a single parent, predominately the mother. In many cultures, the paradigm prevails: *Raising children is a woman's job.* The problem is that women worldwide are broken. Broken women are raising broken children, who grow up to be broken adults, producing a broken society. We must do 'damage prevention.' We must tend the broken hearts of mothers so that they can be whole again and able to produce wholesome children. We must target mothers and mothers to be."

Approval from headquarters came, but with qualifications. "Yes, go ahead and try the idea in Asia Pacific. Come back in one or two years to see what will become of it." What was the qualification? "There is no money in the budget for another new program." New programs are expensive! Several years of research, preparation, and several thousands of dollars had been spent on new programming to reach the youth in the country of Africa, and that program was not yet on the air. She would be on her own and would have to raise the funds.

HOW DOES A NEW RADIO PROGRAM FLY WITH NO MONEY?

Edmund kept encouraging Marlie by saying, "God always pays His bills. He will provide the money." She spent much time in thought trying to come up with an idea to fund the initial expenses she would encounter. She thought she might challenge young families to give up a night of pizza each week and put that money toward the benefit of other families. But God knew that would never be enough for what He had in mind, and He had other ideas.

In faith, Project Hannah was officially launched in Cary, North Carolina, on November 5, 1997, with a kick-off luncheon of fifty-one women. The women listened and responded as they learned how God had opened doors in the New York City area for the Women's Prayer Summit when a few women fasted and prayed on a rotational basis for forty days. Before the close of the luncheon, Glenda Lowell, wife of the president of TWR at that time, spontaneously left the room and returned carrying a calendar on which she had marked off forty days. She passed it around and invited anyone who wanted to be part of this prayer adventure to join. "Write your name on one of the forty days if you want to fast and pray and see what God will do!" It quickly filled up, and that became the first official function of Project Hannah.

Prayer and fasting would become the backbone of the ministry. Ten years later, Marli would say, "We are convinced that *PRAYER IS THE WORK*. Ministry is reaping the results."

To give you insight into what it was like to begin such a ministry, the following excerpt is taken from a fax I received on November 19, 1997, two days after Marli arrived back in Singapore:

"Since yesterday I have been trying to contact the women God has given me here. Several meetings are planned for the end of this week and beginning of next week. We continue praying for more women to be involved and to form the prayer core group here in Singapore. I must confess that God has not given me rest. Day and night I have to pray for this ministry. The faces of women and their situations in this part of the world 'gnaw at my heart.'

"This morning in the local newspaper, I read an article about women and children from the Karen people in Myanmar (formerly Burma). They are called 'long necks.' When little girls are eight, nine, and ten years old, they put metal rings on their necks. Every year they put more rings until there are twenty-five or more, thus leaving these poor women with long necks covered with metal rings. Right now, these women and girls are being stolen from their villages by some men who are using them as tourist attractions in neighboring Thailand. They are being taken from their homes to restore Thailand's tourism industry. Some people are trying to make money keeping these poor women and girls, as the newspaper puts it, 'in a human zoo.'

"All of this is disgusting and very revolting, but the worst for these women and children is the fact that they are already in the hands of someone worse than the men who are holding them in captivity. Satan has had them for generations. He has kept them bound with cords of idolatry, superstition, and fear. How they need JESUS and the Gospel! Since they cannot read and do not have freedom, I'm more and more convinced that GOSPEL

RADIO is the only way to reach them and rescue their souls—to give them hope in a hopeless situation. May God help us to get the message out!"

> NOT BY MIGHT NOR BY POWER, BUT BY MY SPIRIT SAYS THE LORD ALMIGHTY.
>
> —ZECHARIAH 4:6

Marli traveled to Guam the next month to cast the vision of Project Hannah. Eleven TWR women accepted the challenge. A prayer group and a production center were established. Women prayed and God worked.

Remember the group of Brazilian women back in the United States in Newark whom Marli had mentored when she lived in New Jersey during the late 1980s? They did not want to miss out on what God was going to do. As they had been touched by Marli's ministry, they wanted to help other women be so touched. The first offering received by Project Hannah in January 1998 came from these women—$169. Their gift was much like the widow's two small copper coins (Mark 12:42); it came from their housecleaning earnings.

TOUCHING FAMILIES ACROSS THE WORLD

Project Hannah was launched in Singapore in February 1998. A team of twelve women joined the prayer movement. They organized a forty-day rotational prayer and fasting schedule. They prayed for direction and open doors, and their prayer team expanded. They later wrote scripts and donated funds for the programs. They and Edmund served as her "right hand" for as long as she remained in Singapore.

In a period of two months time, eighteen meetings took place on Guam with the Project Hannah *Women of Hope* (new radio program) group and with individuals. This team of inexperienced "radio women" would somehow "get the program on the air!" It would not be an easy task. Many times it seemed impossible, but in less than one year the first *Women of Hope* program aired on October 31, 1998.

Four powerful transmitters blanketed the region from China to Papua New Guinea and New Zealand with the first thirty-minute *Women of Hope* program in English. While the production center was on Guam, the meditation and segment writers, the executive producer, and the final "translation friendly" script editor consisted of three women from Singapore, three from Australia, and three from the United States—all volunteers! To the surprise of everyone, the first listener's letter came from Uganda, Africa. The program had not been expected to be heard in that part of the world.

A year after the first program went on the air, Maggie Fuller wrote, "I have been part of the *Women of Hope* team since January 1998. When we started *Women of Hope* production, we were not prepared to use digital audio and computers. Everything was new to all of us! But God helped us to learn quickly. It is exciting to be part of the team God chose to start such a ministry. He opened the door for me to be the host of this program along with Janette McGurk.

"It is really exciting to know that the work we do here on

Guam [later moved to Miami, Florida] is the glue that connects each program component. We receive features from Singapore, Australia, and the United States. As we sit together here in Guam to make an outline for each program, I am always amazed to see how the pieces seem to fit together perfectly. Obviously, God has His hand leading ours! This is His program. We have produced more than seventy programs to date. It is encouraging to know that men are listening as well.

"We probably receive more letters from men than women. That is most likely because seventy-five percent of all illiterates of the world are women. The letters have been very encouraging. We are touching families! My hope is that these programs will continue reaching the world to touch more and more women in need of hope."

God had been giving others the same hope as He had given Maggie, and they had been responding. God moved people to respond in various ways. The Singaporean team and two donors, one from Germany and the other from the United States, gave substantial contributions that enabled the programming to be quickly expanded. Project Hannah had been launched in Australia and New Zealand. The same month of the pilot program, the prayer movement and the process of production of *Women of Hope* (in their local languages) expanded to Myanmar (formerly Burma), Indonesia, South Korea, and beamed from there into North Korea and shortly thereafter

Cambodia. This required the training of the translators, producers, prayer team leaders, and nonstop travel.

RELEASING EACH OTHER FOR MINISTRY

Remember the newspaper article Marli read about the Karen people in Myanmar, *long necks,* the first week she was back in Singapore in 1997? Is it any surprise that one of the first several invitations for Project Hannah came from there? Isn't that the way God works?

Marli said, "Myanmar was one of the neediest places in the world. While the country claimed to have freedom of religion, the word seeping out reported that the government junta that controlled the people was especially targeting Christians. They were not allowed to fellowship with fellow Christians from other lands. Buddhism dominated with 87.8 percent of the population, and only 3.6 percent were evangelicals."

The new producers of the Burmese version of *Women of Hope* needed to be identified, so meetings were scheduled and everyone was awaiting their arrival. Edmund had promised himself that he would not let Marli travel alone, particularly in Asia, so they had both applied for visas. Marli reported, "The government refused to grant Edmund a visa because he was a media person (no foreign reporters were allowed in the country at that time). However, since I was a 'housewife,' they granted my visa. I was really in a dilemma. A ministry was at stake, yet we were almost paralyzed with fear.

"It was not a safe place to go. Among the few successful export industries at that time were two that were illegal—opium and teak. Yet, at the same time, we felt a sense of urgency.

"Myanmar was one of the poorest countries in the world. Women, of course, were at the bottom of the social order. They were forced to work ten to twelve hours a day in construction sites, farms, and other physically difficult jobs. I was told that many earned just enough to buy eight measures of rice a day, insufficient in most cases to feed their large families. (A measure is equal to a can of tuna fish.) By law their children were put in government day-care centers, where one teacher cared for twenty-five to thirty children.

"We struggled the whole night trying to understand what God was saying to us. Should we stay or should I go? We prayed together for a long time. Around 4:00 A.M., God gave both of us a Bible verse. Our hearts and minds were suddenly flooded with peace, and we decided that I should go. Edmund released me and let me go by myself. That was the beginning of a process of releasing each other for ministry. It has taken several years, but that has enabled us to do what we do. Whenever we can, we travel together. But Edmund still has to bless me, release me into God's hands, and to trust over and over again that he would never be able to protect me as only God can."

On one of her first trips to Thailand, Marli says, "I had traveled the whole day and night to go from Guam to Singapore and from there to Thailand. That amounted to long hours in airports and long delays. I arrived in Bangkok early in the morning and from there went on to Chiang Mai. I had eaten nothing but a few crackers, was totally exhausted, and sick to my stomach. Before going to the guest house close to the organization we work with there, I was taken to the grocery store, and I bought some Melba toast—the only thing I could eat. The guest house was in a compound with several bungalows (Thai style), and I was to stay in one of them by myself.

"I went up the stairs, put my suitcases on the floor, put one of the Melba toast packets on the little nightstand next to the bed, and immediately fell asleep. Later, I suddenly awakened from a dead sleep! Something was crawling all over me! At first I did not know what it was. I looked at the red and brown plaid bed sheets and saw nothing until I realized it was an 'army' of red ants! There were ants all over me, even in my hair. They had discovered my toast and were looking for more in my bed!

"I jumped out of bed and saw three lines of ants coming up the stairs directly to the nightstand with the Melba toast and other goodies. I was terrified! I ran into the shower in the other room, only to discover there were no towels. I had to dry myself with my own clothes. I grabbed my bags and rushed over to find my hostess, who was as terrified of the ants as I had been. She was not happy over my unpleasant reception and quickly found comfortable accommodations for me so that I was able to continue my rest."

> LET US NOT BECOME WEARY IN DOING GOOD, FOR AT THE PROPER TIME WE WILL REAP A HARVEST IF WE DO NOT GIVE UP. — GALATIANS 6:9

The red ants did not deter Marli, and the harvest in Thailand was immediate and continues. A beautiful Thai woman, Dr. Buakab Roughanam, is the voice of *Women of Hope*. Her story could fill another book. "She was born in a small village in the northeastern part of Thailand, near the border of Laos. Her father was a schoolteacher in a remote village, and her mother was a medium. They separated, both remarried, and when Buakab was thirteen, she tried to commit suicide. It was then that she heard about Jesus Christ through an Australian missionary who was tutoring her in English. She gave her life to God when she was sixteen. He enabled her to continue her studies, her educational apex reached when she graduated and received her title of *Dr. Roughanam* from Fuller Seminary in California. In 1998, she was appointed as director of Voice of Peace, a radio broadcasting ministry within Thailand."

Buakab wrote, "Finally, God has answered our heart's cry. I am so glad we can air the Thai *Women of Hope* broadcasts in partnership with TWR. I am more alert to what the Lord has long called me to do—minister to needy women. I am thankful He chose to use a small and insignificant village girl like me to be His ambassador in my country."

Marli said, *"Women of Hope* is not limited to the Thai women. After listening to the program, a Buddhist priest phoned Buakab. He told her he wanted to leave the priesthood and follow Jesus. A few weeks later, he went to the Voice of Peace office in civilian clothing. He told them he is attending a church in the area and is now serving the true God.

"While Thailand is surrounded by nations with repressive governments that are officially closed to missions, Thailand is amazingly open and free. Its people enjoy freedom of speech, of assembly, and of religion. A small but vibrant Church strives to make inroads through the maze of cultural and religious paradigms ingrained in Thai consciousness. I was deeply touched to sense that Christian women, in particular, have a deep concern, even a sense of urgency, to give hope and God's amazing grace and love to their Thai sisters.

"Buakab took me to a place in downtown Bangkok known as the 'Devil's playground.' Thousands of prostitutes work there. Drug sales are rampant, AIDS is epidemic, and much of life is controlled by the mafia.

"We met Susan (name has been changed), an amazing woman with a burning desire to rescue these young prostitutes from a life of misery. She opened a beauty parlor where they come to get their hair styled prior to going to *work*. Tending to their beauty needs are beauticians who once were prostitutes but are now born-again believers. Susan's goal is to rescue women and little girls trapped in sex slavery and to give them a new life. She goes to the brothels and streets and shares the amazing story of God's love. She gives these women the Word of God and health information, but most of all, she gives them hope. Susan embodies Jesus' love. She shines with amazing light and life in Jesus Christ."

Marli continues, "I also met Emily (name has been changed), an elegantly beautiful woman of God, who is fighting a seemingly invincible war. Emily heads the New Life Center in northern Thailand. She left her homeland to serve young teenagers from Thailand's isolated hill tribes who are being sold by their own parents in order to support their opium addiction. She takes these girls in, sends them to school, provides food and shelter, and, with her associates, teaches them skills.

"In the 'House of Love,' Emily cares for girls and young

women who are AIDS victims with no place to go. She nurtures them while they await their impending death. Her compassion and determination to win this war one girl at a time deeply touched my heart, and I saw another point of light in such a dark place."

On a trip from Singapore to Guam over the Philippines, Marli had a long layover in the Manila airport. She wrote, "God has given me a new gift—photography. I pulled out my camera and was taking pictures of women. I saw a group of approximately fifteen young Muslim women. They were all dressed in their traditional dresses with head coverings. The dresses were all made of the same fabric—a calico of green and black. They all looked to be perhaps between fifteen and twenty years old. I asked permission to take their picture.

"None of them spoke English, but by motions and smiles and a word here or there, we understood each other. I 'talked' to the one I thought was the leader. She was beautiful, probably in her late twenties, and tried very hard to communicate. I complimented their dresses, and a couple of the girls came up and hugged me and stroked my face with their hands. However, some of the girls looked sad and scared and would not even raise their eyes. The beautiful woman proudly showed me their tickets and passports. They were all going to Saudi Arabia, and their passports were from Indonesia. I noticed that the tickets were all *ONE WAY*, which made me wonder.

"I heard my flight being called, and I had to run. As I left, they hugged me good-bye, then asked me to take more pictures of them. They also asked for my phone number. As I was going down the stairs, I mused over their *one-way* tickets. *Why?* I wondered? I had just finished reading *The Princess*, and then it hit me, *Are these teenagers being taken to work in restaurants or homes as babysitters OR to 'work' for evil men and to become sex slaves?* If so, they would probably never again see their loved ones. *No return* tickets. My heart broke, and I wept for the possibility that I feared awaited them."

PRAYER IS THE BACKBONE

Edmund was asked to return to TWR headquarters in Cary, North Carolina, in 1999 to assume a new responsibility. Though Marli had grown very close to the Singaporean team, her health challenges welcomed a climate change. It was with great joy that her friends, children, and grandchildren welcomed her and Edmund home again. The ministry would also benefit from her presence in Cary. The unbelievable details required for such a fast-growing ministry had been covered by Marli, various TWR women, and other volunteers. During the next year, Peggy Corcoran was appointed as International Coordinator for Project Hannah. The International Prayer Coordinator's role, vacated by Judy Clauss's changing schedule, was filled by Tina Sessoms.

Marli says, "Prayer is the backbone of Project Hannah. Therefore, Project Hannah seeks to raise a worldwide army of prayer warriors to intercede and stand in the gap for suffering and unsaved women.

"Project Hannah sends a monthly prayer calendar that focuses on women of various countries and each day lists a prayer request. Sometimes, the target is a specific women's issue that goes beyond ethnic and national barriers, such as the girl child, war widows, war refugees, sex slavery, female genital mutilation, etc." Therefore women around the globe are praying the same petition each day.

In addition, each year a forty-day rotational fast is scheduled to end with the anniversary date of Project Hannah, November 5. Participants from around the world join in this time of fasting and prayer. Is it any wonder Project Hannah has grown in such a phenomenal way?

A five-year anniversary celebration of Praise and Prayer for the way God had opened doors and windows for Project Hannah was planned for November 8–10, 2002, in Cary, North Carolina. On November 9, a large assembly of women were invited to gather at a church to meet *Women of Hope* producers from around the world, hear a special speaker, and join together in extended prayer for the women of the world and praise to God for His blessings.

Project Hannah's growth had surpassed every expectation from anyone associated with TWR. The monthly Project Hannah Prayer Calendar was now translated into fourteen languages and represented prayer cells in over sixty countries and territories. *Women of Hope* radio broadcasts in thirteen languages from 120 stations were touching the hearts of countless women, enabling them to discover Christ and experience His peace and grace in their lives despite their daily circumstances.

"LORD, I WILL NOT LET SATAN DEFEAT ME"

Two weeks before the Five-Year Anniversary Celebration, Marli and Edmund were in Brazil. God had opened the windows of heaven and poured out His Spirit upon their meetings in an unprecedented way. After the meetings, they flew a short distance to Curitiba to share their joy with their families and to see Edmund's ailing mother. Never could they have imagined the news awaiting them.

As they walked with smiling faces to the designated meeting area at the airport, Marli noticed her brother coming toward her, but he was not smiling. She stiffened.

"You must call Stacey [her daughter-in-law]," he said.

"Is it Isaac [her grandson]?"

"No."

"Fabio [her son]?"

"Yes. There has been an accident!"

"Is he okay. Is he still alive?"

"No. He was killed two hours ago."

She crumbled into his arms, and Edmund rushed to her side. Words fail to express her anguish and that of Edmund. Only someone who has heard such news could ever understand the depth of grief that engulfed them. Their pastor son—gone! *Why?*

Our God understood their breaking hearts. He knew how they felt as they caught the next plane to the United States.

The stewardess greeted them as they walked onto the plane and found their seats. She followed behind them and asked Marli, "Are you all right?"

"No. I have just lost my son!"

The stewardess expressed her sympathy and went to the front of the plane and soon came back. "There is a seat up in first class. Please come up."

During the course of the trip, the stewardess continued to

stop to talk with Marli and Edmund. She brought blankets and food and insisted that Marli eat so she would have strength to face what lay ahead. The conversation somehow turned to life after death, and Marli and Edmund shared that they knew that one day they would see their son again. The stewardess inquired about their belief. Edmund shared the truth of John 3:16:

> FOR GOD SO LOVED THE WORLD THAT HE GAVE HIS ONE AND ONLY SON, THAT WHOEVER BELIEVES IN HIM SHALL NOT PERISH BUT HAVE ETERNAL LIFE. FOR GOD DID NOT SEND HIS SON INTO THE WORLD TO CONDEMN THE WORLD, BUT TO SAVE THE WORLD THROUGH HIM. WHOEVER BELIEVES IN HIM IS NOT CONDEMNED, BUT WHOEVER DOES NOT BELIEVE STANDS CONDEMNED ALREADY BECAUSE HE HAS NOT BELIEVED IN THE NAME OF GOD'S ONE AND ONLY SON.

As they flew across the ocean, in her hour of deepest suffering, Marli watched as the stewardess knelt in the aisle and confessed her sin (*for all have sinned and fall short of the glory of God, and are justified freely by his grace through the redemption that came by Christ Jesus*—Romans 3:23–24). She asked Jesus Christ to forgive her sins and to come into her life by His Holy Spirit and transform her into a new person. (*Therefore, if anyone is in Christ, he is a new creation; the old has gone, the new has come! All this is from God, who reconciled us to himself through Christ and gave us the ministry of reconciliation: that God was reconciling the world to himself in Christ, not counting men's sins against them. And he has committed to us the message of reconciliation. . . . God made him who had no sin to be sin for us, so that in him we might become the righteousness of God.*—2 Corinthians 5:17–19, 21)

Two weeks later, the night before the five-year anniversary celebration of Project Hannah, Marli got out of her bed that was wet from tears and which had held her since the funeral and memorial service. She dropped to her knees and said, "Lord, I will not let Satan defeat me. I WILL go tomorrow, and I WILL speak of your goodness!"

Over the last five years, Marli has been able to minister to suffering women and men as never before. When she was in a "closed" country to the Gospel this past year, she shared the story of the loss of her son to a group of people.

A gentleman came up and said, "I understand, I lost my son, too." However, this man's loss came because of his belief in Jesus Christ. He would not renounce his faith. He said, "First, they came and killed my teenage son in my backyard. Then they stole all my horses, which is my livelihood. I went to the police, and they told me, 'This is your problem.' Many of us have had our houses burned to the ground. Someday they might come for me." This is the world in which many Christians today live.

"No Matter How They Pray, It Is Okay With Me!"

As the Ten-Year Anniversary Celebration of Project Hannah, November 9–11, 2007, approaches, the Project Hannah team—Marli, Ann, Tina, Peggy and their host of co-laborers—keep asking, "Lord, what do you want us to do in the next ten years?"

Project Hannah has spread in an unprecedented way. It is as if God has flung the Global Prayer Movement, the *Women of Hope* radio broadcast, and the Awareness Program around the globe. At the time I am writing this book, the monthly prayer calendar is distributed to fifty-seven countries in English. From those countries, it is translated into twenty-seven languages and then distributed into a total of ninety-nine countries and territories.

Women of Hope is broadcast in thirty-seven languages over 336 radio stations and is aired 430 times a week. Four new languages are in progress and will be aired when God provides the prayer teams, country coordinators, producers, translators, and financial support.

The programs penetrate walls and veils. Here is one listener's response from North Korea, a country "closed" to the Gospel: "I thank you for your *Women of Hope* radio program that blesses me daily. Through TWR-Korea, I received a radio as a gift. As I listen to your touching broadcast, I feel God's amazing grace and experience my life changing. If that is not enough, I now have comfort in my heart, a renewed sense of hope, unspeakable help, and everlasting wisdom. A blessing such as this must not be kept a secret, so I have told everyone I know to listen to this miraculous blessing. I will continue to faithfully pray that through TWR-Korea, God's gift of salvation will be declared and His kingdom will be expanded."

Marli said, "More than 25,000 Project Hannah intercessors in 99 countries are convinced that *prayer is the work, and that ministry is really reaping the results.* That's what I saw happening at the Women's Prayer Summit. Even before the doors were opened, I saw the earnestness with which several women were 'cleaning' that place, praying in every corner of that building, and claiming it for Jesus. As the summit began, the place was packed with women from all walks of life, all social status, all racial back-grounds, all denominations and religious persuasions, etc. I was a bit concerned in how that huge diversity was going to play out when we actually would bow down to pray together.

"I heard the speaker say, 'Before we start praying, we have some housecleaning business to do. I ask you to turn to the lady at your side, the one behind you, and the other ahead of you. Look her in the eye and say, 'Whatever way you pray is okay with me.' Thousands of women did as she asked them to do. The walls of prejudice and intolerance were broken down in my heart, and I truly believe that happened to most of the women in that theater.

"I just returned from Africa where our Project Hannah inter-cessors all pray at the same time. That does not bother me any-more. They are praying to God, not to me. God is able to make sense of anything He wants, and one thing I know He wants is that His daughters pray talking to HIM. What is His command to us? *Pray without ceasing!*

"I think the prayer summit liberated me in such a way that the Project Hannah prayer movement from its inception has embraced women and men willing to do the work of prayer without ceasing, not dictating that they express themselves to God in a certain way.

"No matter how they pray, it is okay with me!"

AGAIN WE ASK, WHAT CAN ONE WOMAN DO?

WHAT CAN MARLI SPIEKER DO?
Anything God wants to do through her.

WHAT CAN YOU DO?
Anything God wants to do through you!

How to Reach Your City

An Event Planner to Accompany
What Can One Woman Do?

Over the past ten years, I have been asked repeatedly to explain the simple model that the Lord gave to gather thousands of women in the metropolitan New York City area for the prayer summit. God's significant stirrings during those days are still touching lives, and I became convinced that He has directed me to write a "how-to" manual that He will use to glorify His Name.

This manual reduces a complex strategy for reaching people to a simple model and gives a step-by-step formula from the inception of an idea to its concluding event. The model is extremely adaptable by design. It includes ideas and directions for networking, recruitment, fund-raising, ticket sales, and other important steps.

The beauty of this model that the Lord revealed is that it will adjust to any size city (or several cities at once) as well as to an entire state (or several states!). This model is yours to adapt as you seek Him, for He is the One who has revealed this simple yet amazing strategy.

Perhaps God has placed a burden for your city upon your heart that you cannot shake? Are you waiting for someone else to solve the problem? Perhaps **you** are the one to co-labor with our Lord to change the situation! If so, be assured that He will guide each step of the way (Isaiah 30:21), and He is able to use you in unimaginable ways!

If God is calling, *now is the time* to discover what He has for you.

How to Reach Your City is available through Bronze Bow Publishing. You can call for your manual at **866.724.8200** (toll free) or through the Internet at www.bronzebowpublishing.com or write to Bronze Bow Publishing, 2600 East 26th Street, Minneapolis, MN 55406.